The "Sound The Alarm!" Collection

The "Sound The Alarm" Collection

Sound the Alarm, Stand by the Empire and Beware the Money Power

By

A.K. Chesterton

CANDOUR

The A.K. Chesterton Trust

2016

3

Printed and published in 2016. First combined edition.

© **The A.K. Chesterton Trust**, BM Candour, London, WC1N 3XX, UK.

Website: www.candour.org.uk

ISBN: 978-0-9932885-6-2 (Hardback)

This book is dedicated to our great benefactor and patriot, Robert Key Jeffery.

R.K. Jeffery, 1870 -1961.

CONTENTS

Foreword

In October 1954, a British patriot named R.K. Jeffery[1] provided funding for the newly formed League of Empire Loyalists. Part of this funding was used to produce three booklets in the '*Sound the Alarm*' series. They were used to amplify A.K. Chesterton's writings in *Candour*, and establish the policy and ideology behind the League.

The first two booklets have been re-published as part of *The A.K. Chesterton Trust Reprint Series* but this hardback collection contains our first reissue of the third booklet, *Beware the Money Power*[2].

We would like to thank Jeff Carson for proof-reading the text and Tregunta Cathcart for his introduction.

Rob Black

The A.K. Chesterton Trust
October 2016

---

[1] For more information on Mr Jeffery, please see the appendix to this book.
[2] Not to be confused with *The Menace of the Money Power*, dating from 1946.

Introduction

By Tregunta Cathcart

Few, if any, among us today can lay credible claim to the description, visionary. Even rarer are visionaries that prove themselves to be warriors. But there are exceptions, and those that fulfil such demanding criteria deserve to be honoured in the great pantheon of patriots. One of those worthy of such exalted recognition is Arthur Kenneth Chesterton, or 'A.K.' as he was affectionately known. A man of incontestable courage, whose words ring out loud and true, warning us of the dangers we face, both in his own lifetime and down through the generations that he continues to inspire with his call to arms.

And the *Sound the Alarm* series comprising, *Stand by the Empire, Beware the Money Power* and *Sound the Alarm* itself are testimony to the great man's foresight. In a suite of concise and surgical analyses of 20th Century historical events, economic trends and geopolitical machinations A.K. lays bare the inner workings of our supposed representative government, supra-national organizations and the malign influence of Wall Street.

When Chesterton writes of President Roosevelt's 'stance' during the Atlantic Charter meetings of August 1941 being dictated by Baruch, Morgenthau, Frankfurter, Lehmann and Lilienthal, what discerning modern reader cannot see the same process in operation with the hawkish actions of Elliott Abrahams, Paul Wolfowitz and Richard Perle as they guided the gullible George W. Bush into war? Or indeed, the role of Rufus Isaacs, masquerading under the name Lord Reading, borrowing £1,000,000,000 from New York's bankers, on the basis of pay on demand in gold, back in October 1915. Who would make such a deal? Perhaps, someone like Michael Abraham Levy, now Lord Levy, the former chief fundraiser for the Labour Party and a longstanding friend of Prime Minister Tony Blair who managed to obtain a substantial campaign donation from Alexander Bernstein, now Baron Bernstein of Craigweil, with Levy himself being described by *The Jerusalem Post* as 'undoubtedly the notional leader of British Jewry'.

So was Chesterton clairvoyant? Might he be claimed a Nostradamus of the Right? Nothing so hyperbolic. He merely observed and commented upon what others ignored or chose to overlook. After all why would the likes of Jakob Schiff, Kuhn & Loeb, the Warburg Brothers, Otto Kahn and their ilk seek to finance Bolshevik Russia? A.K.'s view was '...because the communist cancer was incubated, not in Moscow but in New York'. With the Vodka-Cola racket being run by the same tribe. The People's Proletariat in the East being overseen by Leon Trotsky (Lev Bronstein), Yakov Sverdlov (Solomon), Grigori Zinoviev (Radomyslsky), Karl Radek (Sobelsohn), Maxim Litvinov (Wallach), Lev Kamenev (Rosenfeld) and Moisei Uritsky. While the Free West was sold an alternative utopia through the silver screen by Hollywood movie moguls like Louis B. Mayer & Samuel Goldwyn of Metro-Goldwyn-Mayer (MGM), William Fox of 20th Century Fox, Jesse L. Lasky and Adolph Zukor of Paramount, Harry, Albert, Sam and Jack Warner of Warner Brothers and Carl Laemmle of Universal Studios.

And the political implications? Well, during the 1990's Jewish oligarchs like Berezovsky, Guzinsky, Smolensky and Khodorkovsky controlled 50% of Russia's economy and were able to asset strip billions under Yeltsin's drunken patronage. And in the West, characters like Michael Bloomberg, George Soros, Sheldon Adelson and Haim Saban fund both the Republican and Democratic Parties in America. Does that go some way to explaining why Benjamin Netanyahu, the Prime Minister of Israel gets 30 standing ovations in Congress?

Having dissected and de-mystified the mechanisms of finance capitalism, Chesterton goes on to shine a bright light on the causes for the demise of the British Empire and the avaricious appetite for the mineral wealth and land mass of her former colonies and dominions. Inevitably, caught in the torch beam of his investigations are the hypocritical instincts of Winston Churchill and Mahatma Ghandi, intellectual insects with egos the size of elephants. Flawed personalities that in a normal epoch would be despised but who's reputations in this ignominious age have merely expanded like a lower colon filled by flatulent gas. It is, to people such as these, that Chesterton rightfully ascribes many of the calumnies of our times. The post-war division of Europe with the betrayal at Yalta, the painful partition of India and the turmoil in the Middle-East.

But it is perhaps with his statement that the *real axis of evil* seeking control over us today wish to ' ...wipe out all traces of national consciousness from the minds of people' that Chesterton reaches the zenith of his wisdom. We all know what he means when he speaks of the 'Americanization of Britain' and we all understand that he is not speaking of the rancher, the factory worker or the cow-hand. Likewise, the logic of his thought and forensic contemplations on the stock market fluctuations of the 1920's and early 1930's could be equally applied to the financial melt-down the world faced in 2007. But that should not surprise us either. For there is a certain similarity between the central actors then and now. Shall we dare to speak their names, in remembrance of A.K.'s fortitude in the face of almost universal approbation? Lloyd Blankfein, Ben Bernanke, Robert Rubin, Timothy Geithner, Gary Cohn, Alan Greenspan and Janet Yellen. And trust me there are many more. The very truth of which should put pay to the canards put forth in David Baker's 1996 biography *Ideology of Obsession: A.K. Chesterton and British Fascism*, that A.K.'s politics were the result of cultural despair and disillusion rather than considered observation. Or indeed, that A.K.'s illustrious cousin G.K. Chesterton was similarly politically incorrect, as per Simon Mayers 2013 book *Chesterton's Jews: Stereotypes, Caricatures in Literature and Journalism of G.K. Chesterton.*

It is to the A.K Chesterton Trust's great credit and an indication of *Candour's* ongoing commitment to keep fighting so that the truth be known that such materials as these are set before you today, in order that you, dear reader, can arrive at your own judgment on such matters. I trust you will not avert your gaze for the evidence is more than merely circumstantial.

Tregunta Cathcart

Lewes
January 2016

SOUND THE ALARM!

A Warning to the British Nations

by

A.K. Chesterton

WHY THIS BOOKLET?

The age of vast empires is not dead. Two of them - the Empire of the Dollar and the Empire of the Kremlin - today command the world. The world on that account is spiritually the poorer. Those who control these huge concentrations of power unceasingly strive to bring the whole of mankind within the scope of international despotism. The British Empire, at whose expense they flourish, does not meet the menace by obligingly crumbling into nothingness. It is necessary for the British peoples and for the world that the British Empire should remain and revive.

This booklet is intended to serve a dual purpose. It will introduce new readers to the policy of *Candour*, the British Views-letter, which espouses the British Imperial cause. Indeed, its contents are the substance of articles published by *Candour*. The second purpose is to explain the motives which have led to the formation of the League of Empire Loyalists, a devoted band of patriots pledged to serve the British future by maintaining a relentless opposition to internationalists intent upon enslaving the world through Communism or through Debt.

Sound the Alarm is dedicated to R. K. J., the animator and inspirator of this new movement.

A.K.C.

EMPIRE IN DISRUPTION

The British Empire is disintegrating. Whoever denies that fact is a fool or a knave. Should objection be taken to such strong language, the answer is that the vogue of the understatement, a quite recent pose, covers with precision the period of our national decline. Great Britain and its world system amounted to something in the days when Britons spoke their minds.

History has never known anything quite as strange as the spectacle of a mighty Empire dissolving itself almost without protest.

In the lifetime of many of us there has twice been witnessed the immolation of the flower of our manhood : millions of gay, brave, unassuming young Britons have been flung into battle to suffer death, wounds, tropical illness, or at best the eating away of their youth—for what purpose? They believed it was for their country. But they were wrong. It was for the eclipse and ruin of their country. In what dictionaries should one search for gentle, soothing words with which to convey what one thinks of that betrayal?

In describing the betrayal of our country, and the betrayal of all the British countries overseas, the present writer has a burning urge to tell his fellow-countrymen, in prose as biting as he can command, about the all-out attack on the British Empire and on Christendom itself which so few of them even perceive to be taking place.

* * * * *

In place of the British Empire, there arises the Empire of the United States. We have no quarrel on that account with the American people, who are entitled to whatever their dollars can buy. Our quarrel is with our own abject leadership, of whatever party, which has supinely allowed the Dollar Empire to grow fat at our expense, crowding us off the stage of history.

When we are tied to the United States financially and economically to the extent that we are now tied to her diplomatically and militarily - the development so devoutly desired by Mr Butler - our Realm will become a mere husk, a facade to disguise the fact that Queen Elizabeth and her people are no longer sovereign in their own lands. We shall be in everything but name the subjects of a cabal of Wall Street financiers.

Indeed, British power is being, or has already been, smothered by her rival over huge portions of the earth's surface. But the vast majority of people in the British world, or what is left of the British world, affect not to notice their national and imperial eclipse. They mouth comforting platitudes about "democracy", "the free world", "the United Nations", " N.A.T.O.", "the European Defence Community", "the International Bank", and the rest, with never a thought that these are power-agencies of the New York Money Trust, which seeks the federation of the nations of the world that it may rule over them as firmly as it rules over the United States Government.

The British people do not know, because no newspaper has dared to tell them, that what they call "American generosity", in the shape of American aid, is in fact the price extracted from the taxpayers of the United States for the establishment of the world-wide Dollar Empire.

And the Dollar Emperor is certainly not President Eisenhower.

* * * * *

Really well-informed Americans know that their own national sovereignty is as much in jeopardy as is our own or that of any of the other grand, historic old nations of Europe. They know that their institutions, national and international, are more or less at the mercy of the International Money Trust, and that great office is accorded only to those who have no doubt where exclusively to look for guidance. Some Americans are even aware that, although Communism is unquestionably trying to undermine the fabric of our society, it is their own Government which smooths the path for the amazing international oligarchy in their midst by pursuing a barely concealed policy of destroying and supplanting our Empire. When percipient Americans make this discovery, surely Britons ought not to look the other way. As one of them put it: "Your issues are our issues, your fight our fight."

The Secret Axis

Should all this seem surprising to some readers, the reason beyond all doubt is that their eyes are fixed on Moscow as the sole source of danger. They have not yet been able to accept the truth that there is a power superior to Communism and Capitalism which frequently uses one or other, and sometimes both, for ends which, were they to be widely enough known, mankind would not for a moment tolerate. This power - let us call it for convenience the International Money Trust - is hostile to concepts such as national frontiers, pride of race, the independence and rich diversity of men, its hostility being based on the knowledge that the spiritual qualities which these concepts enshrine impede its attempts to set up world socialism under a world government—in other words, its own government — and that they contain the ever-present threat of revolt against its authority.

* * * * *

The immediate pretext used for the setting-up of so wide-ranging and exclusive a network of power is the Russian menace. There is no desire on our part to underestimate the seriousness of that menace, which Roosevelt, Morgenthau, Hiss and Co. were so determined should be admitted into the heart of Europe, with consequences now only too apparent.

The vileness of Soviet tyranny never impinged upon the innocent Rooseveltian mind. If it ever impinged upon the minds of his masters, who are still in effective control of the United States, they did not let it deter them from trying to do a deal with the Kremlin. Although for some reason not explained the negotiations for the deal were broken off as early as December, 1945 they went far enough to result in the virtual carving up of the world by Moscow and New York. What is more, should circumstances be propitious, the Money Power would reopen discussions tomorrow for the ruthless completion of that betrayal.

"Protection Racket"

The point which has to be made, however, is that if it be Soviet policy to overthrow the West by force of arms rather than by subversion, the offensive would surely have been taken when there were no more than half a dozen battle-worthy divisions to stand athwart the path of the two hundred Russian divisions massed behind the Elbe. Is it conceivable that the adroit strategists of the Soviet Union would wait for the building up of Western strength before striking? Or are they such simple-minded fellows that the idea of being ringed about in time of war by American atom-bomber bases appeals to the Russian twilight in their souls?

The conclusion is inescapable that the Soviet menace is being used as part of an elaborate conspiracy to reduce the historic nations of Europe to economic impotence and political servitude, and to steal from them the fruits of their long and splendid labours overseas.

As long as the Money-Power is situated in New York and dictates policy to Washington, using the mighty resources of the United States to oust Britain from her world status and make her a financial and political dependency, then so long must we oppose the American nation which allows Wall Street such dominion. If the Devil and the children of the Devil manage to involve us in yet another war, then naturally we shall range ourselves on the American side, because that is inherent in our situation and would be the choice of our hearts as well as of our heads. But to surrender our sovereignty to Wall Street under American duress is a course of action which at all costs we must resist.

* * * * *

In my *Truth* days I once wrote an article suggesting the formation of a body called the League of Empire Loyalists. Its function would be to fight against the internationalisation - that is, the destruction - of the British nations and of the great world system known as the British Empire.

Unfortunately a periodical dependent for its existence upon advertisers and newsagents cannot sponsor a political movement of that kind without placing itself in jeopardy, and the interest aroused by the article at home and overseas could not be canalised. Now, however, the League has been created through the agency of *Candour*. It will soon come into action.

LEAGUE OF EMPIRE LOYALISTS

The tendency everywhere to play down the British *motif* exists because Britain has lost faith in herself and in the star of her nationhood. Let that faith be rekindled and we shall become again a great power, second to none in our influence for good.

If the League of Empire Loyalists develops sufficient dynamism at home, its impulses must radiate in all directions to put heart into our kinsmen over-seas and reawaken in them the knowledge that it is a proud thing to be British.

The proposal is not to create a new political party, but to organise public opinion so as to force upon existing parties policies favourable to national and imperial survival in place of the present policies of national and imperial eclipse.

Make Your Views Count!

Organisation, I suggest, ought not to be top-heavy and elaborate: it should require no large bureaucracy at the centre, but should be kept as loose and flexible as possible. Once the basic principle is understood, the members throughout the country and all over the British world will be able to take and sustain the initiative. Working singly or in groups, according to their preference, their first task must be to keep a vigilant watch in their own constituencies upon Members of Parliament and other public men, to discourage in them their present certitude that the one interest they can safely neglect is the national interest. When internationalist doctrines are expounded on national platforms, the resultant nation-wide protest will very soon compel the politicians, most of whom are careerists and time-servers, to face the realities of an awakened national spirit.

* * * * *

Had a formidable movement of this kind been in existence in 1945 we could not have lost the peace. The United States, instead of waxing great in power at our expense by feeding us with doles and reducing us financially and militarily to satellite status, would today be treating us with circumspection, as allies to be courted rather than as a spent force to be bulldozed into compliance.

Had there been strong branches in Australia and New Zealand, for example, the notorious Anzus treaty, designed to remove these British nations from the British orbit, would never have been signed.

Had there been strong branches in Canada, the separatist policies of Mackenzie King and St. Laurent would have been impossible.

Had there been strong branches in South Africa the futile and craven United Party would never have dared to betray its cause by admitting republicans to membership.

As the League gains in strength it will give particular attention to stopping the rot in the colonial field. The British in India won the warm affection and loyalty of the great warrior tribes and enjoyed the trust of the vast masses of the peasantry.

We were driven out because we disdained to capitalise for political purposes this super-abundant goodwill, but allowed bunches of frenetic babus and pseudo-sophisticates an absolute monopoly of political propaganda and action. Had there been in the British world an adroitly-managed League of Loyalists, it could have acted in the default of the Government of India by organising against Congress the profound pro-British sentiments, not only of the princes whom we betrayed, but of almost the entire population.

Make Yourself Heard!

The same thing could have been done, perhaps could still be done, in the Sudan, where the British Government has again abandoned without a struggle its most priceless asset - the respect and admiration for Britain of the Sudanese people. It may well be that the revival of the British spirit would itself lead everywhere to a revival of loyalty towards Britain. That spirit in decay, however, can lead only to desertion and disintegration.

The first task of the League must be to face the deadly internationalism which makes progressive inroads upon our national sovereignty, and to send it reeling back with a bloody nose. To do that would be to offer battle to the greatest conspiracy of vested interests ever incubated, a task of immense difficulty, and one appallingly complicated by the ease with which the small group of those who seek world power are able to palm off on the masses a spurious idealism which equates internationalism with the brotherhood of man, whereas its true equation is with the enslavement of man.

* * * * *

To get our first clear, authentic glimpse of the policy that is relentlessly being pursued in that conspiracy of vested interests, we have to travel back to the Atlantic Charter meeting. This is what President Roosevelt said to Mr Churchill:

"Of course, after the war, one of the pre-conditions of any lasting peace will have to be the greatest possible freedom of trade. No artificial barriers. As few favoured economic agreements as possible. Markets open for healthy competition... Those Empire trade agreements are a case in point."

Churchill fought back. "Mr President," he said, "England does not propose for a moment to lose its favoured position among the British Dominions. The trade that has made England great shall continue, and under conditions prescribed by England's Ministers."

"You see," replied Roosevelt, "it is along in here somewhere that there is likely to be some disagreement between you, Winston, and me." The argument, lasting some days, ended with Churchill's despairing outburst: "Mr President, I believe you are trying to do away with the British Empire."

Well, there was no doubt about that, except in as far as only the voice belonged to Roosevelt. The brains belonged to Baruch, Morgenthau, Frankfurter, Lehmann, Lilienthal and the other members of the international financial caucus. They had the principle written into every Congressional economic enactment, beginning with lend-lease, and their agents, in the guise of Marshall Aid administrators, later arrived in Europe to stampede us into a progressive acceptance of its implications. Sir Winston has lived to see it all work out, but he gives way no more to lamentations. He seems, instead, to be saying with Bishop Blougram: "I soberly acquiesce." There is - let us be quite clear about this - no question of treasonable intent on his part. The explanation may be no more than that it is always difficult for politicians to believe in the finality, or even the occurrence, of national disaster as long as they themselves have the sensation of steering the ship. Sir Winston, after all his brave words, now presides over the liquidation of the British Empire, but so potent is the alchemy of his mind that no doubt he persuades himself that the process is really one of wafting the Empire to the sunlit uplands of his wartime imagining.

The same excuse, however, cannot serve for some of his followers, who give every appearance of working for the abrogation of our national sovereignty as their supreme political objective.

Many indeed have been the occasions when the nation has been in sore need of a League of Empire Loyalists to keep close scrutiny on the attitude of its own public men.

1917 - AND ALL THIS

When, at the Geneva Conference, Chou En-lai, representing Red China, arose to tell Dulles, Eden and Bidault to their faces that the Western nations must clear out of Asia, there could have been few present who did not hear the flurry of chickens coming home to roost - chickens bedraggled and moulting, but of a size so stupendous that they could not fail to be identified. The only difficulty, perhaps, was to decide the question of their primogeniture.

As a start must be made somewhere, I would suggest that the trouble began in 1917, when the first Lord Reading (Rufus Isaacs) crossed the Atlantic to arrange with his fellow-racials for Great Britain to receive a loan of £1,000,000,000, which she was to repay *on demand and in gold*. As she did not happen to possess that amount of gold, or anything like it, one can readily understand the pressures to which she was subjected - pressures applied with what can only be described as a diabolical foresight. As a result of one such pressure, the British Government refused to renew the Anglo-Japanese alliance, which had been not only a pillar of world stability but a vital British interest.

Had we possessed leaders with sufficient stamina to defy the master usurers, or a patriotic League strong enough to make itself felt, how much more fortunate would have been the sequence of events. We may be quite sure that the renewal aid nurturing of the Japanese Alliance would have made impossible the present spectacle of an arrogant Chinese Foreign Minister serving us with notice to quit the scenes of our labours.

Anything for a Quiet Death

Thirty years later another British Government, this time a government glowing with a sense of its own rectitude, took a further decisive step towards bringing the Eastern - and with it the Western - world to ruin. It liquidated our Indian Empire. What had been a citadel of strength and a guarantor of peace over a vast area became at one stroke a breeding-ground of potential anarchy and the sounding-board for Mr Nehru, adopting the ludicrous pose of an Archangel of Light, to issue directives well calculated to make a shambles of the rest of Asia.

There were swift and dire consequences. We lost Ceylon. We surrendered Burma to chaos. We immensely weakened our position in Malaya. We facilitated the theft of our oil industry and sphere of interest in Persia. We sowed the seeds of the notorious Anzus treaty. That the whole force of American pressure was behind this orgy of surrender cannot be doubted, but the really alarming fact is that no such pressure was needed to set the ghastly thing in motion. The British Socialist Party seemed to entertain the extraordinary thesis that the immemorial power-drives and struggles for survival between peoples had come to an end throughout the world the moment "nice little Mr Attlee" became Prime Minister of Great Britain.

Years of whining and whimpering in innumerable Trade and Labour Councils - unopposed by any organised patriotic opinion - had induced in the new rulers and their sycophants a masochistic frenzy never before known in these islands, but now embracing every party and completing the rot at the core of Churchillian Conservatism.

Orgy of Betrayal

Nor did the British action in Asia stop at self-betrayal. Holland had turned over the whole of her shipping to us during the war, yet for long we denied her the use of her own ships to send troops to rescue Indonesia from the puppet government left behind by the Japanese. At the same time the lamentable Earl of Mountbatten, who later was to rush in where that splendid Briton, Lord Wavell, had disdained to tread and act as midwife to Nehru's India and Jinnah's Pakistan, performed for the Dutch the historic disservice of recognising the

Indonesian rebels as a responsible party fit to negotiate terms with the Dutch Government. Similarly General Gracey, sent to liberate Indo-China, was given a directive so crippling that the opportunity he could have afforded France to reassume full authority was flung away - and flung away in accordance with the deliberate policy of the Roosevelt-Stalin axis, of which the Attlee Government was the enthusiastic stooge.

Now we behold the fruits of that unprecedented orgy of betrayal. Where the momentum of the old British administration has not yet run its course there is still some cohesion. Elsewhere there is bewilderment, illimitable corruption and the shadow of doom. France has fought desperately to ensure her own political defeat in Indo-China. And at Geneva, while the "Great Powers" gave him a respectful hearing, Chou En-lai ordered them to quit what little they have left in Asia.

These home-coming chickens are of the British breed. But there are also American chickens, still larger and more bedraggled, which are returning to roost. The Roosevelt and early Truman administrations were the true creators of Red China. Ringed round with pro-Communist advisers, among them actual Communist agents, and with avowed pro-Russian policies - policies no doubt fashioned by the Red financiers in Wall Street - these enemies of Christendom betrayed Chiang Kai-shek as they betrayed so many of their allies and as they betrayed Western civilisation itself by admitting the Tartar hordes into the heart of Europe. Roosevelt, who was either one of history's most sinister villains or one of her most disastrous clowns, tried to force Chiang to admit Communists to his government, an almost certain method of expediting the Communist march to power.

After Roosevelt died, Truman - or Baruch and the Kuhn, Loeb gang, whichever you please - sent Marshall to continue the pressure on Chiang, while on the Lattimore level the Wall Street and State

Department Reds were busy undermining Chiang's regime, softening it up for Mao's victory, which Roosevelt had already assured by double-crossing Nationalist China in a secret agreement with Stalin about future dispositions in Manchuria. Americans, as they received reports of Chou En-lai's speeches at Geneva, must surely have had long, deep thoughts about Roosevelt, Hopkins, Marshall and the whole Red-operated apparatus of their wartime and immediate post-war regimes.

* * * * *

Side by side with the American pro-Russian policies, revealed in the notorious memorandum Marshall took with him to Quebec, were the American anti-British and anti-European policies, framed to reduce our power, weaken our sovereignty and destroy our empires and overseas spheres of influence, preparatory to their annexation by the Dollar Barons.

These policies persist, but an angry American uprising has put an end, at any rate for the time being, to the identification of the United States Government with Communist aggrandisement. Instead, advantage has been taken of the international ferment to consolidate "American" power over the non-Communist world in Europe and Australasia and to build up in Asia a huge Wall Street vested interest which pays far bigger dividends than the former secret accord with Moscow. More American technicians and advisers are now in Pakistan, for instance, than there ever were British officials in that country.

Even more significant was President Eisenhower's declaration of the United States interest in Indo-China, which was not to help its French ally but to maintain a free trading area for Japan, now an American colony and repository of many billions of dollars invested there by Kuhn, Loeb and the other New York international lending houses. Yet now that this part of the Dollar Empire is threatened, the Lords of Cosmopolis, through their governmental agents, not only force upon

France the relinquishment of her sovereignty in Indo-China, but demand that Frenchmen fight and die for a cause which, so far as France is concerned, no longer exists.

Where in history can one look for a comparable blend of cynicism, impudence and self-interest? The Money Power, now sure of itself, has thrown off all restraint. It treats the nations of the world as cattle. It will not thus treat us when the League of Empire Loyalists throughout Britain and the Empire begins to provide a lead for the patriots of all Christian nations, large and small.

TRUTH ABOUT COMMUNISM

Critics of *Candour's* stand for the national sovereignty of the British peoples against incessant American pressures always base their argument on the supposition that such resistance must aid the Soviet Union. They find incomprehensible our assertion that the opposite is the truth, that as the breaking down of normal tissues provides the conditions favourable for malignant growth, so does every impairment of the principle of nationhood make us the more vulnerable to the cancer of Communism. The belief that the United States affords protection against this danger, whatever may be its momentary truth, is historically false, and it is false not only because America seeks to break down healthy national cells as part of her nominal anti-Soviet policy but also because the Communist cancer was incubated, not in Moscow, but in New York.

Let doubters read with close attention the sixth of President Wilson's Fourteen Points, presented in an address to Congress in January, 1918: —

"The evacuation of all Russian territory and such a settlement of all questions affecting Russia as will secure the best and freest co-operation of the other nations of the world in obtaining for her an unhampered and unembarrassed opportunity for the independent determination of her own political development and national policy and assure her of a sincere welcome into the society of free nations under institutions of her own choosing; and, more than a welcome, assistance also of every kind that she may need and may herself desire. The treatment accorded Russia by her sister nations in the months to come will be the acid test of their goodwill, of their comprehension of her needs as distinguished from their own interests, and of their intelligent and unselfish sympathy."

That was a most amazing piece of special pleading. As American public opinion, then as now, was wedded to the system of private enterprise, it is clear that in thus furthering the cause of the bloody-handed, anti-Christian revolutionary terrorists President Wilson was not speaking for the American people.

For whom, then, did he speak? The answer is - for the men who plotted and financed the revolution, men who - so far from being the horny-handed sons of toil of the popular imagination - were the international financiers at the heart of the New York Money-Trust. Prominent among them were Jacob Schiff, the Warburg Brothers, Otto Kahn and some of the European affiliates of their international banking firm of Kuhn, Loeb and Co. It was this same complex of interests which had used Wilson to sponsor the creation of the Federal Reserve Board system whereby they gained control over the entire credit mechanism of the United States and became the effective secret government of that country. The same financiers accompanied the President to Versailles, dominated his actions there, and campaigned with the utmost vigour for their "Russian" protégés, then amiably engaged in exterminating their Christian opponents by the millions. I put the word "Russian" in quotation marks, because in truth the makers of the revolution on Russian soil were of the same race as the financial backers of the revolution in Wall Street. These "Russians" using every imaginable kind of fraud to defeat the immigration laws, had swarmed into the United States towards the end of the century, and by slick brains, energy, cohesion and abashless self-confidence had made themselves the biggest and wealthiest pressure group in the land. The British Ambassador, Sir Cecil Spring-Rice, placed on record their power to dictate American policy during the First World War. They were a state within a state, using their host's physical means to serve their own purposes all over the world.

* * * * *

When Wilson fell in the great American reaction, the political influence of these Lords of Finance steeply declined, and for many years they were compelled to rely upon other countries - our own among them - to serve their special racial purposes, foremost among them being the nurturing of their Soviet foundling and the preparation of the ground for the rape of Palestine. When Roosevelt came to power in 1932, however, they re-conquered the United States. Incidentally, they made prodigious fortunes out of the New Deal.

The outbreak of the Second World War found them again in a position to take over the secret government of that country and to pursue much the same sinister policy. America did not enter the First World War until Czarist Russia was overthrown, or the Second World War until Hitler attacked Stalin's Russia. Once the Berlin-Moscow axis was shattered, however, the Wall Street cabal swept to its revenge, in the process almost openly organising the United States as a part of the great Finance-cum-Communist conspiracy against Christendom.

Specially protected Reds were placed in key positions, where they evolved the policy which was fulfilled when the Russians were admitted to the heart of Europe and given their heart's desire in the

34

East, and when the decision was taken for the United States to share the post-war world with the Soviet Union - which would assuredly have happened but for Stalin's inexplicable withdrawal from the plot at the end of 1945 - at the expense of Great Britain and the other Western European nations. Innumerable instances of the conspiracy could be furnished, but perhaps none so clear-cut as that provided by General Mark Clark, who tells in his autobiography how, as the Allies pushed back the Germans in Italy, the formidable M. Vyshinsky, with the full knowledge of the U.S. Government, travelled in their wake to try to organise the eventual Bolshevisation of Italy.

From UNO to World Revolution

Even while the war was still being waged the policy-makers of New York, using as tools Red agents such as Alger Hiss and Harry Dexter White, brought into being the United Nations as the basis of a projected super-state and the World Bank as the basis of a projected international credit monopoly. They also created U.N.R.R.A., the two-fold purpose of which was to bolster the economies of the new Soviet satellite states in Eastern Europe, where almost all the relief was distributed, and to finance the illegal migration to Palestine. So blatant had the policy-makers become in the pursuit of their designs that Mr Henry Morgenthau, then Secretary of the United States Treasury, even sent the Russians plates so that they could print their own dollar notes.

No more alarming picture of internationalist power exists than that of the seizure of Palestine, carried through under the direction of international officials armed with the diplomatic immunity which all countries, including our own, were coerced into extending to United Nations and U.N.R.R.A. personnel. There was scarcely a government which was not suborned to play an active part in the infamous proceedings. The picture was first given to the world by General Sir Frederick Morgan, European head of U.N.R.R.A., who related how train-loads of prosperous refugees, with pockets stuffed with money, were allowed out of the Russian-controlled regions to take part in the illegal trek. There had clearly been a bargain between Zionist headquarters and the Kremlin to secure this result. General Morgan was finally dismissed from his post for daring to affirm that U.N.R.R.A. was also functioning as a Communist espionage organisation, his quietus being delivered by New York's La Guardia.

* * * * *

So unblushingly has history been falsified before our eyes that most people accept without question the idea that the era of the great American loans began when Washington decided to line up the West against Communism. That is pure fiction. The original proposals included an initial loan of £1,500,000,000 for Russia and Marshall Aid, so far from being an anti-Communist measure, was intended - until Stalin withheld his co-operation - to be fed to countries behind the Iron Curtain.

When the American reaction set in, as it had set in after Wilson's solid support for Russia at Versailles, the master-planners of Wall Street, paying the time but needful woe, concentrated upon building the West into their system through N.A.T.O. and its related bodies, cashed-in upon the seventy billion pounds worth of rearmament orders which followed the outbreak of the Korean War that had been contrived through the deliberate withdrawal of American troops, continued to work for "one world" - their world - and they now await a favourable opportunity of openly reuniting the anti-Christian forces of New York with the anti-Christian Soviet Union.

That policy-objective outlined in Wilson's Point Six has never been dropped. Capitalism and Communism, in terms of power, are merely their twin-mechanisms to destroy the sovereignty of the Christian nations and merge them into the projected super state, where the Money Power will exercise full sway and masterdom through that monopoly of atomic energy which is being sought with such feverish and fiendish persistence.

When the pall of death hung over Hiroshima, the great mass of mankind thought of it in terms of human agony and desolation, but the few - the very few - whose minds took no account of such things thought of it in terms of power - their power. Scarcely had the evil cloud drifted away before the monopolists were seen to have staked their claim to become the masters of this most fearful magic.

It was no accident that atomic energy control in America at once passed into the keeping of the interests which exercised power, not only over the previous master-weapon - which was gold - but also over the United States Government. What is more, had American public opinion not been roused, the secret of nuclear fission would officially have been passed to Moscow, so that if world monopoly were not accorded the policy-makers as a result of their Western power, they might still acquire it through their power in the East. Advance information, together with fissionable material, had already been sent to the Soviet Union by that mysterious White House figure, paid by nobody knows whom, named Harry Hopkins.

Super "Gangster Stuff"

The Congressional decision to ban the sharing of atomic secrets in no way diminished the zeal of the crusade - if that be the word - to secure "international" control of this new source of masterdom. And there was never any doubt as to the financial and racial identity of those who proposed to be the masters.

The plan announced by Mr Bernard Baruch would have given to a small body, no doubt consisting of, or designated by, himself and his cronies of the New York cabal, absolute control over deposits of fissionable material in whatever part of the world they might be located, over their mining, their storage, their processing and their ultimate use. There has never before been witnessed a more blatant or a more outrageous attempt to dominate mankind by cornering the materials of power - power not only over the economies of the nations, but over their actual physical existence.

The grand strategic end was the World State, marshalled by atomic police in service to International Finance.

"Eisenhower's Idea"!

I have written "was," but the plot, unhappily, does not belong to the past: it is perhaps at this moment reaching its greatest intensity of endeavour. Consider this fact. When the Berlin Conference was mooted at Bermuda during the Eisenhower - Churchill meeting, skilled hands were manipulating the strings behind the scenes, with the result that the President flew back to announce to the General Assembly of the United Nations "his" scheme for the establishment of a world bank of atomic energy.

Admiral Lewis Strauss, of the good ship Kuhn Loeb & Co., informed his fellow-countrymen a few weeks ago that President Eisenhower had given long and profound thought to such a project. That is as it may be. What would seem to have more relevance is that twenty-five years ago, when only a Major in the United States Army, Eisenhower made the one and only move of his career which history will describe as brilliant - acting on sheer inspiration, this obscure officer sought and obtained the advice of Mr Bernard Mannes Baruch.

Never was any step so richly rewarded. Baruchian influence later lifted him over the heads of one hundred and fifty of his seniors to place him at the head of the Allied armies in the West. After the War Baruchian influence placed him in cold storage at Columbia University, until the time was ripe for Baruchian power to make him President of the United States. And now Admiral Strauss, present chairman of the U.S. Atomic Energy Commission, has the charming innocence to ask us to believe that it was Eisenhower, the simple soldier, and not his patron and benefactor, who conceived of the idea of a World Atomic Bank. The secret of the masterdom of the Lords of Baruchistan is that they use every sort of camouflage to disguise the fact that they relentlessly pursue purposes which easy-going Christendom imagines long ago to have been dropped.

Something Special

The timing of the Eisenhower announcement and the method of its presentation were designed to carry the suggestion that the World Atomic Bank was all part of the Berlin peace move. Indeed, it was during the Conference that discussions for the Bank's establishment began between the United States and the Soviet Union. Why these two countries should be regarded as the twin foundation-stones of the revived scheme for atomic monopoly has not been explained, nor is it likely to be explainable except in terms of that sinister polarity which I have endeavoured to show. It is sufficient to note that the atomic talks did not falter when the Berlin Conference faltered, or break down when the Berlin Conference broke down. Nor were they affected by any of the U.S.-U.S.S.R. clashes at the Geneva Conference. They were something very special, these talks - something truly supra-national. Suspended at the moment of writing, they will assuredly be resumed.

Lords Over All

While they are proceeding, Admiral Strauss works overtime, and with an almost comic obsequiousness, to praise the sublime wisdom of President Eisenhower in having initiated them. The propaganda-backing is world-wide. And no wonder. The stakes are immense.

Imagine the industries of all the nations a few years hence driven by atomic energy supplied by the World Atomic Bank, because that is the essence of the proposal. Then imagine the overwhelming disaster to any national economy which, in the event of potential disobedience, would follow the cutting off of such supply.

It is for that power to cut off supplies that the leaders of the International Financial junta work with relentless purpose. Once it is theirs this world in its totality will belong to them. Admiral Strauss, of course, exudes enthusiasm from every pore as he tells mankind of the blessings which will accrue once the plan is accepted. The altruism, the passionate love of their fellow-men, exhibited by the members of the cherubic firm of Kuhn, Loeb & Co. is such as to warm the heart.

The Emperor Baruch, while lending the authority of his own voice to the splendiferous promises of the good Admiral, continues to stress the more rigorous aspect of the plan - control. President Eisenhower's proposal, he told a New York audience - generously giving credit where it was not due - "will be a worthy endeavour if it succeeds in widening peaceful atomic uses", but it could not take the place of "a truly effective, enforceable system of international inspection and control".

Mr Nehru, whatever else may be said of him, at least had the courage to show his awareness of the plot. The American proposals, he pointed out:

"envisage an international control agency which will be set up by the United Nations but will be independent of the world body. This control agency, according to the U.S. proposal, will have guards in the territories of other countries and also power to give or withhold licences to countries and people for purposes of production or research in atomic energy. Such a body will in fact become a super state, maintaining its own guards or army. The proposal means concentration of tremendous powers in the hands of the select body."

What the Indian Prime Minister proclaims today was asserted seven years ago by two British publicists who, working independently of each other, had reached the identical conclusion. One of the publicists was Mr Douglas Reed. The other, if the claim may be made with seemliness, was the present writer.

Both had long been students of the technique used by the Lords of Misrule.

Admiral Strauss would be very scornful of any doubt being cast upon the motives behind the "Plan". He tells us, indeed, that it is intended to allay apprehension about the atomic future. I do not know whose fears it stills. It greatly accentuates my own.

The "Russians", or "Poles", or "Germans" who have conquered America seek also to conquer us. They have already, under cover of our alliance, in large part destroyed the British Empire. That is why *Candour* proclaims the need for a great British revival and a British Declaration of Independence. We are being blinded by the alliance, with its fiction that our destroyers are our protectors.

They are nothing of the kind. They will sell us into slavery as willingly as they will sell into slavery the American people upon whom they now wax fat and whose material resources they use for their own nefarious world-wide purposes. To say, as some say, that in exposing their plans for world dominion we are playing the Kremlin's game is to act as an unconscious agent of Christendom's betrayal.

The tragedy is that although the facts I have narrated are well known to an increasing number of people in the United States, there is almost total ignorance of them in the British world, where even to mention them is to conjure up in sleepy, complacent British minds a sense of the preposterous - and consequently to be adjudged mad.

The facts nevertheless remain facts. Nothing has been written here which cannot be proved. Fortunately the conspiracy has not yet fully succeeded. Whether or not it does succeed depends in large part upon our capacity to warn our fellow-countrymen of their danger, because only the retention of British sovereignty and the restoration of British power can ensure to the world that stability which will save mankind from the appalling tyranny of the proposed all-embracing Centralised Police State.

As things are, our people are lulled by Communist deposits lost at the polls. That is not the kind of Communism we have to fear. Communism is not a movement of poor men, but of rich men - the richest men in the world - and it does not need Communists in the British House of Commons to bring us crashing to the ground.

That aim is achieved by attacking our national sovereignty, in which cause Members of Parliament, forgoing their brains, only too often lead the van.

LEADERSHIP WANTED

Although their heads are undoubtedly confused, the instincts of the mass of British people are not yet decayed. Given forthright British leadership, there could not possibly be found a more essential, a more popular, a more inspiring cause than a national and imperial revolt against all the sinister internationalist enemies who beset us, determined that we shall be transformed from proud Britons (those of us, at least, who are still proud to be Britons) into a cosmopolitan rabble, herded and driven by the leaders of the internationalists who frequently in their own newspapers and meetings proclaim this to be their supreme objective. The fact that few Parliamentarians dare to espouse the popular cause of Britain is a frightening tribute to the power of the unseen opposition.

Conservatism is so smug, so entrenched in self-esteem, so lacking in conviction or principle, that only an electoral demonstration on a wide enough scale that "patriotism pays", that there really are "votes in it", would call back the Tory hounds from vying with Labour and Liberal hounds in pursuit of the internationalist hare and send them off upon the worthier course of national survival.

Politics and Bread and Butter

Does this seem too harsh a generalisation about Conservative Parliamentarians? I do not think it is very wide of the mark. Some are better than others, of course, but take them all in all they are a poor, tame, gutless bunch, prepared to be all things to all men, always sheltering behind smooth but meaningless catchwords. One or two have said to me: "My dear fellow, you should realise that we do much better service by not making a public stand. It is in committee that the real work is done and there, we assure you, we make our voices effectively heard."

I was more impressed by that argument three or four years ago than I am now. Although the Empire is falling apart in the flabby, nerveless hands of the Conservatives at as fast a rate as it was given away by the Socialists, there have been only one or two protests from those whom some of us have supposed, too charitably, to be the custodians of the imperial cause. As we are dragged along at the cart's-tail of New York our independence as a nation is being steadily destroyed. We hand over without a murmur our spheres of influence in Greece, Turkey, Egypt, Persia and Pakistan to our supplanters; and if dissident Tories in the privacy of committee are indeed kicking up a row about the perpetual surrender it must be a very decorous row, so decorous as to be completely futile. "Now do be reasonable," they will say to me. "What do you want us to do - break up the Party?" They fail to explain where lies the profit in preserving the Party and losing the Empire.

The truth is that Party warfare today, even more than when Belloc and Cecil Chesterton exposed it, is a pitiful sham-fight. Its moves have become as stylised as the conventions of Chinese drama.

Treason Must Not Pay

The real political issues, thanks to the dewy-eyed enthusiasm of some or the supine defeatism of others of our Members of Parliament, cut across Party-lines and reveal themselves as mere differences of opinion upon the manner and the speed with which we divest ourselves of our age-long national independence, and transfer our terrestrial loyalty to a "higher" authority than Her Majesty the Queen - a junta whose visible members might well be Dulles, Eden, Spaak, Mrs Pandit, Major Salem and Uncle "General China" and all! That adherence to some form of greasy internationalism should have become a shimmering political objective for every British political party is the measure of our fall.

Whether or not a new party would be any better than the old parties, one thing is certain: the nation cannot long continue on its present basis of spiritual treason. Because it is treason, beyond doubt it is treason, to dissipate the heritage of a thousand years; destroy the values which those thousand years have seen created, and prepare to hand over the sovereign right to our obedience to the people who are putting up the money for "World Government " - that is, to the World Governors Designate, the would-be masters of mankind who are indifferent whether their tyranny is implemented by international financial sanctions or by the Arctic labour-camps so long as no such "anachronism" as a sovereign national state is left to challenge the absolutism of their power.

* * * * *

On the question of how a national revolt might be organised, and the fruits of victory achieved and preserved, a recent public opinion poll disclosed that a majority of those taking part no longer had confidence in the Conservative Party, or its leader, to save the British Empire from extinction. It is good to find men and women breaking loose from the hot-house atmosphere of high-pressured propaganda and facing facts. What should they do next?

Nothing is easier than to start a new political party. One man in a room has only to declare himself to be the president or secretary or whatever it may be of such an organisation, and to give it a name, for a new party to exist, even though it may expire the same day. Many dozens, perhaps many hundreds, are born every year. The significant fact, however, is that in our nation of fifty million souls only three parties enjoy electoral support, and of these three one is being inexorably squeezed out of the arena.

Thus the inescapable conclusion is that, though the birth of a political party presents no problem, to nurse it through its teething troubles is perhaps the most difficult task possible to imagine. Most parties, for all practical purposes, are still-born. The infant mortality rate among the rest is about 100 per cent. Here and there a group struggles on in almost total obscurity for a few years, to die without having made the slightest impact on the country's political life.

Those who talk of starting a new party should ask themselves how they propose to secure for it immunity from the common fate. But that does not mean we are without means of defence and counter-attack.

There is no Internationalist Party, yet every party is rotten with internationalism. The reason is that the internationalists have captured all the key positions, including the B.B.C., Chatham House and even the political columns of many newspapers which are supposed in the popular imagination to represent quite a different point of view. I have particularly in mind Mr H. V. Hodson, editor of the *Sunday Times*, Mr Alistair Forbes, political commentator of the *Sunday Dispatch*, and Mr C. S. Melville, diplomatic correspondent of the

Evening News. These are internationalists serving Conservative newspapers, and surprising though it may seem the vast bulk of Conservative opinion still believes that the Conservative Party is the champion of a sovereign, independent Britain. Conservatives have not yet realised that it is almost as completely the handmaiden of internationalism as any of its rivals in the amicable shadow-fighting of Westminster.

Now nobody really supposes that in the breasts of the sturdy sons and daughters of Britain resides any exorbitant love of alien influences in their public or commercial life, or that they long for their terrestrial loyalty to be transferred from Her Majesty the Queen to some cosmopolitan cabal functioning as a supranational government in New York or Tel-Aviv. It just happens that small groups of very clever propagandists contrive to misrepresent the prevailing climate of opinion in the image of their own designs. What has to be done, therefore, is to secure a hearing for the authentic voice of Britain. Is there any reason why we should not profit from the example of our adversaries?

This is where the League of Empire Loyalists re-enters the picture. There is being brought rapidly into being an organisation of British patriots which will raise such a hornets' nest under any public man who dares to speak or act against British sovereignty as to put him in fear of his political career.

The organisation will not cut across a patriot's positive political creed: given good faith he can belong to any party or group, or to none. By supporting the proposed vigilance movement he will help to ensure the retention of a country in which to work for the fulfilment of his own beliefs. Men may have legitimate differences of opinion as to how to cultivate their garden, but if in the course of quarrelling about it the garden is filched from under their noises, who but their despoiler profits?

* * * * *

The immediate task is the defeat of the enemy and the liberation of the British genius that it may again assume the leadership of mankind, a role that in the long run depends less on quantitative considerations (American dollars or Soviet manpower) than on quality. British morale in the past has been incomparably great. In an age full of the atomic menace, it is certain that the only weapon which can stand up to the atom bomb is the weapon of morale.

The desperate need is unity. The League of Empire Loyalists therefore fights on the sole issue of national and imperial survival. But too much emphasis cannot be placed on the fact that the League, instead of competing against bodies whose aims of social and economic reform require the retention of national sovereignty, can only give them powerful background support and ultimately a vast recruiting ground.

Enough has probably been written to show why, in facing the illimitable dangers which threaten our historic nation, we do not give a more particularised support to constructive policies. When the house is on fire, its occupants - at any rate those of the British breed - do not normally fall out about the rebuilding or the refurnishing until the flames have been put out.

Unfortunately only a few intellectually alert Britons to-day understand that the national house is ablaze.

That is why we have made it our own task to sound the alarm. We seek the help of our fellow-countrymen. Once their ears are reached and their eyes opened, we are convinced their hearts will not fail.

STAND BY THE EMPIRE

A Warning to the British Nations

by

A.K. Chesterton

WHY THIS BOOKLET?

This booklet is the second in a series intended to serve a dual purpose. Through these booklets readers will be introduced to the policy of *Candour*, the British Views-letter, which espouses the British Imperial cause. Indeed, the contents of this booklet are the substance of articles published in *Candour*, and of other articles written by the same author for other publications before *Candour* came into existence.

This series will also make clear the reasons which have led to the formation of the League of Empire Loyalists, and the aims of this devoted band of patriots who are pledged to serve the British future by maintaining a relentless opposition to internationalists known to be intent upon enslaving the world through Communism or through debt.

The *Sound The Alarm* series is dedicated to R.K.J., the animator and inspirator of this new movement.

A. K .C.

THE BRITISH EMPIRE'S DARKEST HOUR

"The age of vast empires is not dead. Two of them—the Empire of the Dollar and the Empire of the Kremlin—to-day command the world. The world on that account is spiritually the poorer. Those who control these huge concentrations of power unceasingly strive to bring the whole of mankind within the scope of international despotism. The British Empire, at whose expense they flourish, does not meet the menace by obligingly crumbling into nothingness. It is necessary for the British peoples and for the world that the British Empire should remain and revive."—

From *Sound the Alarm*.

There could be, for British peoples, only one disaster worse than the dissolution of the Commonwealth; that would be their own lack of awareness of the fact. Such a happening, in an age captivated by slogans and formulae, is possible. The modern British are developing a passion for praising fictitious relationships and pretending that all is well where all is ill. The sooner the deception is dropped, the sooner will the nation be able to see the way ahead with clearer eyes. We could, for example, go on for years, in increasing subjection and misery, talking about something that had ceased to exist. That is why we should look behind the Commonwealth facade to ascertain whether the inside is in good repair. The investigation may not produce very encouraging results, which makes the task more urgent.

I have long been convinced that the destruction of the British Empire, and the abandonment of national sovereignty in favour of a supranational junta of power-addicts, is the dominating *motif* of modern world policy, and that the would-be world-governors have now manoeuvred themselves into a position where they can use the wealth of America's all too innocent taxpayers to finance the entire conspiracy.

This hour of darkest doubt is nevertheless the hour of greatest opportunity. Such is the precariousness of the party balance that half a dozen Members of Parliament who really believe in Conservatism could act as the arbiters of our country's destiny and the guarantors of its future greatness.

* * * * *

There is no doubt that the vast majority of British people all over the world would enthusiastically endorse a policy that reasserted this country's sovereign greatness, but not one political leader of any present significance shows the slightest disposition to sound the reveille. Some have recently stopped gathering posies in the international field, and begun to speak in friendly fashion of Commonwealth and Empire trade, but much more is needed than the sort of outlook which regards a British world economic system as an expedient to fall back upon whenever multilateral trade fails to meet our needs. The spirit is all-important.

Sir Norman Angell, who in his day has championed causes by no means always prompted by considerations of national and imperial survival, has come belatedly to the stool of repentance. In the hour of what may prove to be its disintegration, he finds that, after all, there is something to be said for the British Empire. He contributes to the *Daily Mail* an article which contains this striking passage: —

"The most tragic recent consequence of our indifference to the moral case for Empire arose in the military strategy adopted towards the end of the second world war, imposed by American opinion and feeling. Franklin Roosevelt was a warm friend of the British people, and helped Britain in the early years of the war more than we can ever repay, yet he regarded the British Empire as an evil and malign conception, and insisted that the later strategy of the war should be based on the assumption that the post-war world would have less to fear from Russia's power than from Britain's."

That is, at least, part of the truth, although not the whole truth, and even in certain respects false. "American opinion and feeling" imposed no military strategy. Except in as far as it is acted upon by a powerful few, the mob is deaf and dumb and impotent: it imposes nothing. Nor was the decision vested in Franklin Roosevelt. That is why I need waste little time disproving Sir Norman's ridiculous assertion that Roosevelt was "a warm friend of the British people." Friendship, indeed, is a queer name to give to a policy aimed at the betrayal of a staunch war-time ally.

Such help as was organised did not derive from any love of British eyes, but because World Jewry had decreed the destruction of Germany.

Roosevelt was one of the chosen agents of that work, and—although less consciously—of the related work of building up the power and influence of the Soviet Union.

No Interests Of Our Own?

One of the things which vitiates the British spirit is the fantastic convention of these times that we must not even suggest upholding our own national and imperial interests without apprehensive glances across the Atlantic and a headlong rush to explain that those interests are at one with American interests. This sort of sentimentality does not appeal to intelligent Americans, and its cumulative effect on the British spirit will surely be lethal.

The *Daily Mail*, in a leading article discussing Sir Norman's contribution, picks upon the American magazine *Time* as an exponent of this continuing anti-British bias. "Week after week," it writes, "this journal manages to work in something about our forthcoming dissolution—and always as though rubbing its hands over a corpse. Why—we do not know."

Considering that the entire American policy is directed towards the furtherance of that dissolution, the singling out of *Time* might seem a little strange, if not comic, but at least it offers an opportunity of supplying the explanation which the *Daily Mail* confesses itself unable to provide and about which Sir Norman Angell is discreetly silent.

Dwight D. Eisenhower was Bernard Baruch's nominee for the United States Presidency. No informed person, I think, would dispute that fact.

President Eisenhower's Administration sent to Rome as American Ambassador Mrs. Luce, another political protégée of the powerful Mr. Baruch.

When the present writer was editing *London Tidings* a furious letter came his way from Mrs. Luce threatening to do damage to that publication's circulation in the United States because of some comments he had made on Baruchian policies.

The good lady claimed to be deep in the great man's political confidence. And the husband of Mrs. Luce, as I need scarcely add, is the proprietor of *Time*.

Is it far-fetched, therefore, to suggest that the relish with which *Time* anticipates the downfall of the British Empire is shared—to put the matter no more strongly—by Bernard Mannes Baruch?

Let us investigate.

The passionately pro-Bolshevist Administration of President Wilson —let anybody who questions this description re-read the Fourteen

Points—gave Mr. Baruch a position whence he could yield such immense leverage as to be able to boast to a Congressional committee that he was the most powerful man in America. *Is it fair or unfair to assume that the most powerful man in America had some means of making his influence felt in the drawing-up of the Wilsonian pro-Bolshevist programme?*

First Germany Then Britain

During the Roosevelt years, before and during the war, the world was given a pleasing picture of Mr. Baruch, the "Elder Statesman"—sometimes called the "Uncrowned King of America "—sitting on the park bench and pondering the advice he would give when summoned each day to the White House.

Mr. Walter Lippmann, in a moment of quite remarkable candour in 1932, asserted that Roosevelt was not his own master, but was used by others. Who exercised the real masterdom? Perhaps Mr. Baruch would know.

The "Elder Statesman" never took any steps to dissociate himself from the popular belief that he was a man who profoundly influenced White House policy. Is it fair or unfair, therefore, to assume that he "shared" President Roosevelt's assumption "that the post-war world would have less to fear from Russia's power than from Britain's?"

Was he, by any chance, an accessory before and after the pact of Yalta? Of course he was.

When a correspondent, after the war, mentioned to Mr. Baruch Britain's desire to maintain Imperial Preferences, he replied with a magnanimous gesture: "Why, we'll let the British keep their Preferences. We'll let them keep the Preferences for three years."

"And after that?" enquired the correspondent. "If they still want the Preferences we'll extend the term by another three years," replied the bountiful Mr. Baruch. Nobody seems to have asked what powers were vested in this Wall Street tycoon that he should cast himself for the role of Providence, able at will to sustain or destroy a great empire.

In 1946, while the Foreign Ministers were meeting in London, Mr. Baruch arrived with a mighty flourish, announcing through the Associated Press that he had come "to hold the big stick over the Big Boys, to make damn sure they do not foul up the peace." Who would be more potent than the Governments of the victorious allies? There can be only one answer—the International Money Power, operating from New York.

* * * * *

The International Money Power, using the United States Administration as its chief instrument, was the malignant force which financed the Bolshevist Revolution and pleaded for it at Versailles.

The International Money Power was the malignant force which, some 25 years later, brought the Red Army into the heart of Europe.

The International Money Power was the malignant force which greatly preferred the Soviet Union to the British Empire, and it remains the malignant force which has carried forward the work of destruction to the point where Mr. Baruch's friend, the proprietor of *Time*, rubs his hands "as over a corpse" at the thought of our demise.

The Americans have every right to their own foreign policy. What Britons have no less right to object to, however, is the idea so often propagated by our leaders that American interests inevitably accord with British interests. There is a general assumption that the United States wishes to preserve the power and glory of the British Empire, whereas the truth is that she wishes to supplant that power, and is rapidly achieving that ambition.

She has seized all the dominant military, naval and air force commands.

She has relentlessly assailed and whittled down Britain's Imperial Preference system.

She has engaged in some very queer political manoeuvres at our expense in Persia, Egypt, Greece and Turkey.

She has excluded us from pacts made with our overseas kin.

There is no sense complaining of these moves, but it would be unforgivable not to see them, and gross cowardice not to counter them in the interests of our own survival. The adulation which some of our public men of all parties slobber over America is not only disgusting —to the better Americans no less than to ordinary British people— but, in its effects, it is a betrayal of Britain. It is calculated to suggest that our future is secure in American hands, which is a perilous fallacy.

THE SURRENDER TO WALL STREET

It is a sombre thought that while the Left—or a big section of it—advocates the cession of the British Empire to Moscow, important elements of the "Patriotic Right" should counter-attack with the proposal that the surrender should be made to New York. Still more sombre is the thought that such a policy can be put forward by the greatest newspapers in the land with absolute certainty that there will be no public demonstration, no slightest hint of outrage from our ancient nation, once proud and virile and full of splendour.

Rarely has there been a more shameless example of sheer grovelling sycophancy than Mr. Nutting's defence of the American Government against the charge, brought by Mr. Enoch Powell in the House of Commons, that it is using its influence to destroy the British Empire.

The dispossession of the Anglo-Persian Oil Company, if not instigated by American interests, was upheld by them and by the State Department, even before the event occurred.

After the war, New York financiers, acting, under cover of the International Bank and other agencies, set out upon the economic conquest of the earth. The huge American surplus was to be used to drench the nations with dollars and soften them up for the slaughter.

Persia was included in the programme, not only because of its oil and untapped mineral wealth, but because as a British sphere of influence it had to be subverted and its pledged word destroyed.

The new conquerors did not propose to tolerate Britain's political and economic rivalry here or anywhere else.

When the International Bank moved into Persia it took with it a private American concern called "Overseas Consultants Incorporated," whose function was to spy out the land and discover means of infiltration into the Persian economy. "Anglo-Persian" could scarcely have liked the development. General Razmara, the pro-British Prime Minister, certainly did not welcome it.

Exit Britain...

When the extent of the new activities became apparent he cancelled the licence granted to "Overseas Consultants." That was to challenge the greatest power on earth. Who can doubt that the decision was taken there and then to clear the British out of Persia?

Not long afterwards General Razmara was assassinated. Events moved with a speed quite foreign to the indolent East. Almost at once Moussadek succeeded to the Premiership and introduced into the Majlis a bill for the nationalisation of the oil industry. The solemn Persian pledge not to take this step before 1991 was cynically flouted. "Anglo - Persian" was cheated of the fruits of its labours in one of the most scandalous international robberies of modern times.

Great Britain, in close treaty relations with the United States, asked for Washington's support. The response was a few mumbled words which the British Press proclaimed to be a protest against the Persian action. Then Moussadek made a revelation which would have shocked into awareness any people less doped than our own. *He let it be known that before embarking on nationalisation he had sounded Washington and been assured by President Truman that the United States policy towards the dispossession of the British would be one of neutrality.* In other words—" Go ahead, my boy, and good luck to you."

* * * * *

Other facts then emerged. Mr. McGhee, at that time the State Department's Middle Eastern expert, had been in Teheran the week before the gigantic robbery took place, and had given the Moussadek Government all possible encouragement. Immediately afterwards Ambassador Grady began a propaganda campaign to reassure the Persians that they would not be left financially in the lurch. In the middle of the dispute Mr. Averill Harriman went to Persia as President Truman's special envoy to tender his good offices—if that be the term—as mediator between the contending parties. He had not even left the airfield on his arrival in Teheran before telling reporters that, whether or not Persia reached agreement with Britain, American aid would still be forthcoming.

And the supine British Government took it all without a murmur of protest. Our oil-men were withdrawn from the concessions. There began a kind of siege of our great refinery at Abadan. Mr. Herbert Morrison, at that time Foreign Secretary, sent warships to the Persian Gulf. For a dazzling moment it seemed as though the balance might be redressed. But it transpired that the Royal Navy was to be used only to help in the scuttle. Mr. Morrison lost Abadan for us, but boasted to Parliament that he had kept his own head. The nation would have been the richer had the process been reversed.

...Enter The World Bank

Even this did not satisfy our supplanters. Soon every British consulate in the country was closed down. British trade with Persia was brought to a standstill. To crown all, diplomatic relations were broken off. The debacle was complete.

What next? Mr. Henry Morgenthau, fugleman of international finance, was quick to provide the answer. He suggested—as though the thought were quite a casual one—that the International Bank might be induced to take over the Persian Oil industry as a going concern.

The International Bank indicated that it would be happy, out of sheer altruism, to comply with that request. It sent a mission to Teheran.

But the pace had been rather too fast and furious, the move too blatant. Some more months were allowed to elapse before the proposal of setting up an international consortium to work the nationalised oil industry, with funds provided by the International Bank, was revived.

Then there was another development. Moussadek, either on his own volition or on instructions from the New York bosses, plotted the Shah's overthrow. As the Money-Power is consistently opposed to Monarchy, it is not improbable that it wanted the power of the Persian Crown destroyed. But Moussadek now over-reached himself. There was a counter-revolution which encompassed his own downfall and restored the Shah.

As the Shah, with an enterprising young British reporter in attendance, entered his plane at Rome to return to his country, an order came from Teheran: "No British." The young reporter had to leave.

"No British." That remains the watchword. The Shah, no less than Moussadek, had had to toe the line. Whoever rules in Persia now does so by gracious consent of the Dollar Barons.

Our entire sphere of influence in Persia has been taken away from us.

Washington and not Whitehall now calls the political tune.

Our immensely wealthy oil concessions, pledged to us for the next fifty years, have been filched.

Our great refinery at Abadan has been stolen.

The future of the industry will be determined, not by the City of London, but by Wall Street.

Dollars already flow in to sustain the Shah as previously they had flowed in to uphold his traitorous Prime Minister.

And the depths of our humiliation are reached when the British Government, in the mood of a licked cur, puts up the egregious Mr. Nutting to fawn upon the United States and thank it for the help it has given us in Persia! That surely is the abomination of abominations.

Lords of East and West

No more profoundly revealing example of the surrender to Wall Street can be imagined than the revolutionary change in power-politics about to take place in the Mediterranean. The acquisition by the United States of strong naval and air bases in Spain means that the Western Mediterranean will become an American sea. General Franco, surviving the pressure of many months, has managed to retain the principle of national sovereignty over the selected areas, but although the concession pleases Spanish pride, and is a tribute to his own personal character, the victory is only nominal—once the Americans are ensconced in Spain, it will take more than decrees of the Spanish Government to shift them.

Simultaneously with the reaching of an agreement with Spain came the announcement that Washington had signed a pact with Athens. This provides for the "sharing" by the United States of Greek naval and air bases, which are to be enlarged for the purpose. The Greek Prime Minister said that strong American forces would soon arrive in the country to take up their stations. In other words, the new Lords of the Western Mediterranean are also to become the Lords of the Eastern Mediterranean.

What of the Central Mediterranean? As Italy has long been a satellite of the New York Money-Power, it might be thought that the United States had this area, too, nicely tied up. But there seems to have been one fly in the American ointment—a remarkable little fly called

Malta. From the British point of view—if such a thing can now be said to exist—what is happening to Malta is the crux of the entire revolutionary situation in the Mediterranean.

First it is necessary to recollect that as the Americans moved into Spain and Greece, so did we begin to move out of Suez and the Sudan. The State Department covertly, and American-inspired organisations openly, have been as successful in undermining our influence in the Nile Valley as they have been in collaring our spheres of influence almost everywhere else in the world. In consequence we have to remove our 70,000 troops from the Canal Zone and thus end the chapter of our splendid service to Egypt, the Sudan and the whole civilized world.

We might expect to hear, in consequence, of the transfer of units from Suez to British possessions, which are few enough, in the Mediterranean. We might expect, in particular, a strong British air reinforcement of Malta. Instead, what do we find? We find in the instant of our expectation, the strong *American* air reinforcement of Malta. We held that island throughout the war. Why should it be supposed that we are no longer capable of holding it today without the help of American squadrons? Why should Americans be moving not only into Spain and Greece, but into Malta? It is difficult to believe that the British Government which permits this thing is a free agent. One would prefer the explanation that it acts under duress.

Stars and Stripes Over Ethiopia

In 1941, before the United States entered the war, British Empire troops in a series of swift advances defeated the large Italian army in Abyssinia and restored the Negus to his throne. Has Great Britain benefited from that most signal service? Not in the least. The Anglo-Ethiopian agreement, on its expiry, was not renewed, the British military mission was withdrawn and the number of British advisers drastically reduced. Reaping as always where they have not sown the

Wall Street vampires have sent their minions to take virtual possession of the country freed by British military achievement.

Reuter has reported that all the principal advisers in Ethiopian ministries are American, that they have access to top secrets and influence decisions, that Ethiopian Air Lines Inc., is an American concern, that the State Bank of Ethiopia is managed by an American, and that with the Yanks have come "dazzling features of Americanism" such as limousines, jeeps, films, gaudy shirts, neckties and chewing-gum. Britain is completely "out." The present writer, who sweltered in the vanguard of the advance into Abyssinia, often wondered what benefit his country would derive from such exertions. Now he knows, and the knowledge is not sweet.

"American" designs upon Abyssinia clearly have not stopped with the ousting of the British. The Emperor Haile Selassie, among whose titles is that of Conquering Lion of Judah, has himself been conquered by Judah—that section of it which rules the New York roost. There seems very little doubt that his prolonged visit to the land of his new masters had the two-fold purpose—in conformity with the now all too familiar pattern—of further enmeshing Abyssinia in debt to international finance and of granting military and air force bases to the United States Government. Indeed, it is clear that the country is to be the foundation-stone of the American Empire in Africa.

* * * * *

Washington and New York, taking advantage of the vast economic strength at their disposal, and also of the pitiful weakness of the post-war British Governments, have been instrumental in driving us from the fruits of our military, administrative and pioneering labours all over the world.

It is they who have done most to sustain the tainted propaganda against "colonialism," the system which alone can stand between vast numbers of the human race and a reversion to outright barbarism. Yet the "Americans" do not blush to supplant it with their own, utterly indefensible imperialism, which is being spread throughout the earth by the simple process of buying governments for spot cash.

If Great Britain cannot be prevailed upon to emulate the example of Portugal and make a stand in defence of her overseas territories, the barbarism of the future will be no less hideous than the barbarism which she suppressed in the past because it happens to disport itself in gaudy shirts.

Dr. Salazar, by standing firm in defence of Portuguese territory in India, completely called the bluff of New Delhi. The Indian Government had openly sponsored a spurious movement purporting to represent the alleged ambition of the Goanese peoples to unit with India. A comic-opera "liberation army" was mustered with a view to marching upon Goa and smothering it by "non-violence." The Portuguese awaited the event with steady nerves, and eventually a tiny trickle of dispirited youths—all that materialized of the "liberation army"—appeared on the scene to wave a flag and tamely to submit to the authorities. [3]

What a light that episode shed on the British scuttle from India! As the overwhelming majority of Goanese are content with Portuguese rule, so were the hundreds of millions of ordinary Indians happy and content under British rule. The Indian agitation was as much fabricated and as empty of real substance as was the "Goanese" agitation. But, instead of standing firm and relying upon the loyalty of Indians to the Crown—a loyalty displayed on all the battlefields of the world—the craven British Government surrendered to the clamour of frenetic demagogues and abandoned the whole vast country to the tender mercies of its grasping landlords, usurers, political chancers

---

[3] India resorted to force to conquer Goa in 1961.

and murderous thugs. To think that we once spoke disrespectfully of the Portuguese!

India did not, as a result of the Attlee-Mountbatten scuttle, become free of external influence. All that happened, apart from the battering to pieces of about half a million people, was that New Delhi lifted its eyes from London to Washington and New York. Missions from the World Bank and the Fourth Point administration have been roaming all over the vast sub-continent to take an inventory of its resources. They will soon be in effective command. Nehru thinks he has placed bounds upon what he calls American "controlism." There never was so optimistic a view.

* * * * *

As the result of an Act of the United States Congress Washington is to have an elaborate Gandhi Memorial occupying an eight-acre plot on a hill overlooking the city. It now only remains for India to erect a mammoth statue of Mr. Bernard Baruch towering over New Delhi for reciprocity in kind to be achieved. Reciprocity in other ways has long been established, since it is the custom of the ruling oligarchy in both countries to pat themselves and each other on the back, claiming for both nations an exalted spiritual destiny which sets them apart from mankind.

Mr. Nehru often refers to the United States as a pioneer in blazing the trail of "freedom from colonialism," while Vice-President Nixon, during his recent visit, not only returned the compliment but endorsed the tributes paid to the United States. Typical of his utterances was this gem: "I am proud to represent a nation that throughout its history has championed the cause of freedom for all people against exploitation and foreign domination. You may be sure that American tradition has not changed."

No doubt the Vice-President's hearers were suitably impressed. As, indeed, they should have been. The fight waged by the United States against the foreign domination of the North American Indians belongs to history. Even so, perhaps here and there some who listened to Mr. Nixon, remembering that the population of India has increased almost beyond reckoning during two hundred years of beneficent British rule, found themselves wondering how many—or how few—North American Indians have survived to testify to United States championship of "the cause of freedom."

One or two scholars who know a little history may even have felt like asking their distinguished visitor how it came about that California, New Mexico and Texas were acquired by his countrymen. He would have replied, it may be, that these were the legitimate spoils of a war waged against that formidable Fascist power, Mexico.

The Saintly Ones

While they claim to be actuated only by motives of pure spiritual grandeur, the United States and India are two of the most materialistic countries on earth. India since the withdrawal of the British has become saturated with corruption at every level and corruption is materialism in its most practical form. The United States is proverbially the land of the "almighty dollar." Its present world empire, which Mr. Nixon has been inspecting, has been bought far less by blood than by dollars, and most of it represents conquest not over enemies but over friends and allies whose war-time and post-war plight it has shamelessly exploited.

Nothing could be more fitting, therefore, than that the United States and the Republic of India should unite to do homage to quite the most fraudulent "saint" and preposterous "hero" of modern times. The tricky lawyer and the unscrupulous politician combined with the vapid visionary to make of Gandhi a colossal clown—a clown whose folly cost at least half a million lives. He was the preacher of non-violence who lacked the mother-wit to perceive that violence on a prodigious scale would be the only end of his doctrine. The advocate of handicrafts and the simple life, he had not the gumption to understand that by creating modern nationalism in India, which had never been a nation, he was paving the way for all the distempers of Western industrialism and financial tyranny that the World Bank and the Fourth Point Programme boys are now foisting upon a helpless Indian people. He was the sweet, truthful soul whose speeches had only one refrain: "Get rid of the British and all your miseries will vanish." If he believed his own claptrap Gandhi was a madman; if he did not believe it he was a liar.

Had Gandhi really loved his people he would have kept them within the protection of their only true friends, the completely honest and disinterested Britons of the Indian Civil Service and of the Indian Army. Instead, he handed them over to a noisome bunch of babus who will land them in eventual anarchy. He was the most irresponsible leader ever to win the plaudits of the multitude, being far more concerned with his own vanity than with the lives of his followers.

Nobody reading his correspondence with Lord Linlithgow during a crisis of the war can fail to remark that it was the British Viceroy who had the sense of responsibility becoming to his office, while Gandhi showed himself to be a mean-spirited, snivelling little egoist utterly indifferent to the suffering which his attitude must inflict upon the masses. Finally he "fasted unto death" with a regularity which became tedious and yet contrived to live for over seventy years under British protection. That is the real, derisive comment upon his life's work.

* * * * *

By way of compensation, Gandhi is to become a leading deity in the Washington pantheon. Why? For one reason only—to mark the hatred of the British Empire which animates the American nation. Mr.

Nixon's boast about his country's alleged championship of freedom was uttered in the same cause—to do us moral damage in the hope of filching from us yet more of our heritage.

Indeed, the Vice-President, when he reached Karachi, was even more explicit. He said that he was "fully conscious of the fact that Pakistan had started from scratch." One has only to think of Britain's engineering feats, and of the administrative, legal and military heritage she left the Pakistanis to denounce that statement as a damnable lie. He said that "the American people have great love and respect for the people of Pakistan because Americans and Pakistanis are animated by the same ideals. You cherish your independence and your freedom. You know what it means. You recognize the old colonialism from which you have come to independence should not be returned and you would not want its return".

Let us see this for what it is — blatant anti-British propaganda. If we had a Government worthy of the name, instead of the present dollar-hungry, lickspittle crew, it would create such an uproar in Washington about Nixon's behaviour that the United States Government would deeply ponder the advantages of treating its principal ally with at least a minimum of respect. The British withdrawal from N.A.T.O. — if seriously threatened—would so gravely jeopardise the plans of the policy makers that we could command some modification of the abominable American attitude towards us.

* * * * *

We can say little about the impending American deification of Ghandi, however, when the British Government—which has responsibility for the Kenya Government —is doing precisely the same thing. The Board of Trustees of the Gandhi Smarak Nidhi (Gandhi Memorial Fund) have sanctioned a grant of Rs. 15,000,000 to the Gandhi Memorial Academy at Nairobi, which — incredible as it may appear—has been sponsored by the joint efforts of *the Kenya*

Government and the Indian settlers there. The trustees express the pious hope that the academy "will be able to help better understanding of the Gandhian philosophy". Moreover there is to be an official move to introduce a Bill in the Legislatures of Tanganyika, Uganda and Kenya giving the academy statutory recognition in East African territories.

Kenyatta Next?

Have we British lost all power of reason? Is there some suicidal urge at work within us? Gandhi's "non-violence", as I have said, cost more than half a million lives in India: how many will it cost in Africa once there is "better under-standing of his philosophy"? That we should officially pay tribute to the man who systematically defamed us, who worked for our ruin, and who had to be locked up lest his activities should assist the Japanese to conquer us, is beyond words damnable. It is an encouragement to the Kikuyu to expect the ultimate deification by the British of Jomo Kenyatta, and to every other tribe to rebel against the British authority.

Hidden Treason At Work

The explanation may be no more than that another loathsome attempt is being made to ingratiate ourselves with Nehru, which surely marks the lowest depths to which it is possible for a once-proud people to sink. But whether or not it be conscious, there is no doubt that there is a kind of treason at work deep hidden within our political life. Unless we can root it out, we must expect the Nixons to cock a snook at us as they rush about the globe arranging for our disappearance from world history.

RECORD OF DISASTER

John Bull enjoyed the respect of our fathers because he insisted upon British sovereignty. He was master in his own house, and he held that house inviolate. Much might be wrong there—much, indeed, was wrong—but there was nothing wrong that lay outside his power to put right.

He was in the act of putting things right when Cosmopolitanism arrived to overthrow him, to trample upon his values, to debase his traditions, to replace his native aristocracy by an alien plutocracy, and to divide the people of England, who had stood together through the vicissitudes of a thousand years, by means of the hideous doctrines of the class war. Thereafter it was only a matter of time before national sovereignty came to be frequently filched from his countrymen, and before the national way of life began to lose its quality and become a crooked and boggy track leading to national dissolution. Sir Winston, despite his contrary assurance, presides over the process.

We have crashed from world masterdom to satellite status with possibly irreparable damage to ourselves, but without making any appreciable dint in the armour of Churchillian complacency. Not a single sentence has escaped his lips to suggest awareness of the British tragedy.

Sir Winston, it may be, has fallen a victim to his own legend. His inordinate pride in his war-time fame may have made him incapable of supposing that things can go far wrong as long as he has charge of our destiny. This is not written out of disrespect for the man, but out of anger and pity that our great nation should have made such prodigious efforts, and twice in thirty years have suffered such appalling losses, only to bite the dust as a result of policies which were essentially his own.

The entire British future—the future of the infants now in their cradles and of their children and their children's children—is being betrayed. Their heritage is being recklessly dissipated. And it's happening under the auspices of Sir Winston Churchill. It is happening, indeed, with all the more ease because of the massive personality which cushions the impact of each successive disaster upon the public consciousness.

"Massive personality"—nobody will deny that to Sir Winston. But it is not a synonym for wisdom, or even for adequacy. The adequacy of a statesman must be judged by the fruits of his statesmanship, and the Churchillian fruits — let us bravely face the truth—are to be sought amid the debacle of our national and imperial fortunes. Rather than entertain so rank a heresy, the more fervent of his admirers will bid us look at his war-time services. Those services should be acknowledged. Our morale was at a low ebb when Churchill took over in 1940. But should that crisis ever have arisen?

Our British world might still be intact had we allowed Germans and Russians to fight themselves to a standstill on the desolate Steppes. The entire Hitlerian build-up was for the *Drang nach Osten*. That it turned into the *Drang nach Westen* was the work of international finance, aided by a British war party which used demonic energy to push this country, unprepared as she was, into a terrible war exhausting to her strength, long before Germany and Russia had exchanged a shot. Who was the leader of the war party which so blithely hazarded our national existence? Winston Spencer Churchill.

When the panzers were streaming into Holland and Europe's long nightmare had begun, Winston Churchill became Prime Minister of Great Britain. He has told us, in a confession as frightening as it was candid, that he had no need of happy dreams that night, because "some things are better than dreams". The thought of the agony of Europe, it seems, could not prevail against the thought of the triumph of personal power achieved. Historians in search of evidence about Churchill's fundamental seriousness—or fundamental levity—must surely brood upon that piece of self-revelation.

Roosevelt's Lieutenant

Nothing from that day to this seems to have undermined the man's soaring confidence and self-esteem, although to be able to soar has required in him at times something akin to split-consciousness. At the Atlantic Charter meeting, for instance, he became aware of how unscrupulously the United States intended to make use of its power of economic leverage; he accused Roosevelt of seeking to destroy the British Empire. Yet before long he was proclaiming himself proud to be the "lieutenant" of this same man who worked for our ruin.

Almost everything for which Churchill stood was derided by events. He upheld the principle of the integrity of Poland, yet was obliged to acquiesce at Teheran, when the decision was taken to dismember that unhappy country. He later rounded on the protesting Polish Prime Minister and told him that he should be sent to a lunatic asylum for endangering allied relationships. Churchill also stood for the containment of Communism, yet was obliged to acquiesce at Yalta, when the decision was taken to extend its sway to the River Elbe. He said further, that he had not become Prime Minister to preside over the liquidation of the British Empire, yet he traded British bases for antiquated American destroyers, sent out the Cripps mission to prepare for the surrender of India and generally proved so impotent to control the deluge he had helped to set in motion that when the war ended with the victory of our arms, we were economically too exhausted and spiritually too drained of energy to take advantage of it.

Yet although the Eastern barbarians were then in the heart of Europe, although we had been reduced to a position of virtual subservience to foreign powers, and although the British Empire was brought to the verge of the abyss over which much of it has since fallen, Winston Churchill's thoughts were kept in water-tight compartments to such an extent that on the day of victory he set out to give himself the ecstasy of a popular triumph by visiting in turn each of the Allied Embassies and receiving the tumultuous acclaim of the London crowds. He had found it a good war, an enjoyable war, and he was profoundly pleased with himself.

* * * * *

It is probable that Churchill, even when he realised precisely what had happened to Europe, saw no connection between the ruin of its greatness and the policies he had so strenuously pursued. It is almost certain that when he went to make his speech at Fulton he thought of himself, not as one whose policies had led to colossal disaster, but as a renowned world-statesman, whose efforts had met with glorious fulfilment—even if the fulfilment had brought the Russians to the Elbe.

What Churchill said at Fulton set the stage for all that followed. The affairs of Britain, he said, must become mixed up with the affairs of America. He would not stop the process if he could. And now the entire non-Communist world, instead of being an alliance of sovereign, independent nations, has been forced by fear and economic duress into a system of military command such as Rome never dreamt of and Britain never thought to achieve. Americans rule the seas, the land, the air. They are the bailiffs of high finance, whose dread sanction is the withholding of dollar aid. We have triumphed over the terrors of great battles only to beg and whimper for our dole.

Obediently—under Mr. Attlee—Great Britain crawled out of India and Burma. Obediently she gave the franchise to near-savages in

Nigeria and the Gold Coast. Obediently — under Sir Winston Churchill — she now places Malta at the disposal of the American air force, prepares to withdraw our fighting troops from Egypt, and ignominiously allows shabby little international commissions to supervise our withdrawal from the Sudan. The child being father to the man, what would the Lieutenant Churchill who charged at Omdurman think of the Sir Winston who throws away sixty years of British toil and loving care?

There are some who associate Sir Winston with an occult plan to bring all these things to pass. That seems to me to be the sheerest nonsense. I do not believe it for a moment. Such a plan does exist: once or twice, when off-guard, Churchill himself has caught a very clear sight of it. But that he himself wills its fulfilment is a thesis fit only for the brain of a madman. Although he has served some queer causes—the restoration of the gold standard being among the queerest —I am quite certain that there is some corner of Churchill's heart that is forever England. But it is overlaid. Overlaid by the glee of his own renown. Overlaid by the acclamations of a world which mistakes oratory for statesmanship. Overlaid beyond hope of allowing him a clear understanding of what havoc his life's work has wrought upon the land he loves.

The trouble is not that Sir Winston is actuated by any sinister motive — he certainly is not — but that his fame is a mighty facade which conceals from his own gaze, as from the gaze of his fellow-countrymen, his own lamentable inadequacy to cope with the world he has helped to bring into being—a world dominated by Washington, New York and Moscow, in which Britain is being systematically robbed of every vestige of independence and power.

* * * * *

President Eisenhower not long ago paid a timely visit to Canada, where he addressed both Houses of Parliament. If, as Head of the

American State, he showed any awareness that the Head of the Canadian State which received him was Her Majesty Queen Elizabeth II, the British newspapers regrettably neglected to inform their readers of the fact. The President took what might seem to be the opposite line. He spoke of the United States and Canada as "partners". He even referred to them as "equal partners". Evidently—to adapt Orwell — some partners are more equal than others.

The idea that Britain might be in a relation of partnership with Canada perhaps escaped the President's mind. He made no reference to her in this context, perhaps thinking that she was adequately covered by the phrase "our friends in Western Europe". This blatant attempt to pull Canada still further away from the British orbit into an American "partnership" is all part of long-standing policy, but that it should be done by the President himself on Canadian soil shows how far international manners have shared in the general decay of our times.

The mission undertaken by President Eisenhower in Canada had its counterpart a week or two earlier in the mission to Australia and New Zealand of Vice-President Nixon.

Mr. Nixon was admitted to meetings of both the Australian and New Zealand Cabinets, as a sign of the close and confidential relationship established between Washington on the one hand and Canberra and Wellington on the other. No doubt the word "partnership" was often on the Vice-Presidential lips. The master-idea, of course, is to set up a system of political and economic consultation from which Britain will be excluded as firmly as she is from the Anzus Treaty.

American tactics are more fully revealed by the Congressional politicians who make a point of visiting the British Dominions to preach the gospel that Britain herself is finished. Forty years ago these insolent busybodies would have been tarred and feathered, or ducked in the river. Their behaviour would fully warrant such treatment.

Consider, for instance, the theme of Senator Ellender, who told the good people of Auckland: "The United Kingdom should by all means possible transfer her great know-how where natural resources are abundant — Canada, Australia and South Africa—and not try to make a come-back in the British Isles. There is no hope of that. Britain has no natural resources except coal and iron ore."

He said that U.S. aid to Britain was being used more or less to maintain her tottering economy, and went on: "Most Commonwealth countries are now wearing long pants and are taking from the United Kingdom much of the business she once enjoyed. I have been told that the sterling pool is being used to the advantage of the United Kingdom. Many Commonwealth countries and colonies are not getting their fair share of the American dollar pool."

That was not only political bounderism of the most reprehensible kind, but sinister propaganda for the birds of prey whose beady eyes are already fixed on what they suppose to be the decaying body of the British Empire. That the citizens of Auckland did not drive Ellender from the platform may well have been because the palsied leaders of Britain appear to share his view. It would not be surprising were he asked to address the British Houses of Parliament on the same theme.

* * * * *

When Cairo denounced the Anglo-Egyptian Treaty its first step was to expel all British technicians from Government employment. As they came out, the Truman Fourth-Point boys swarmed in, together with missioners from the World Bank, the Export-Import Bank and every other conceivable and inconceivable American agency. £200,000,000 was allocated by the World Bank for Nilotic developments, but the money was withheld pending —pending what? It is not difficult to guess the answer. The unified control of the entire Nile waterway. And what did this entail? The booting of the British from the Sudan. Hence the smile on the Dulles face when this was achieved.

Yet presumably the British people will continue to adore and revere supine leaders who have been outwitted at every turn. Why? Because there is just about as much reality in the British electorate's choice of a blue rosette as there is reality in a naked Dinka's choice of a spear instead of an elephant or a butterfly to represent him in the parliamentary stews of Khartoum.

The Conorada Petroleum Company of the United States has been given by Egypt an oil concession contract for an area of 114,000 square miles bounded by the Mediterranean on the north and the Libyan frontier in the west. The concession is granted on exceptionally favourable terms. No rent on the prospecting areas retained during the first twelve years is to be payable, while after thirty years the contract is to be renewable for another thirty years. American capital since the war has been pouring into Egypt in such a flood that it is now virtually impossible for any other nation to secure rights comparable to those contained in the oil deal. Egypt has become an American financial satrapy, and Col. Nasser, strut as he may, would not hold his position for a split second were Wall Street to decide upon his downfall.

So swift an economic conquest has been possible only by securing the elimination of British influence in Egypt. Although we rescued the country from the clutches of the old corrupt Ottoman Empire, gave it good government and defended it against the Axis powers, our American supplanters have no compunction in reaping where we have sown. That is the way of the world and our anger should not be against them but against our own leaders, of whatever party, whose careers have consisted of incurring for us an unbroken record of disaster.

THE IMPERIAL THEME

Because of our neglect of the Imperial theme, and the sorry impotence of our general world policy, influences which have already robbed the Crown of India and Burma have been at work in Canada as also in Australia and New Zealand, hostile to the British connection. If Britain can now emerge from her pitiable plight and act again as a resurgent Power, the hearts of men and women of British blood all over the world will rise to her with one accord, and their leaders will be forced to drop what often seems to be their present policy of jettisoning British associations and traditions in return for toothy inter-nationalist smiles.

When Rome began to totter, those who were the most privileged, and therefore who owed her the most duty, were the first to dissociate themselves from the processes of her disintegration. Withholding from the Romans the leadership which birth and position should have made obligatory, they retired to their villas and left their fellow-countrymen to their own devices, praying that the structure would last their time but stirring no finger to keep it in repair. They were decadent.

How would the Britons of the still privileged classes like to hear themselves similarly described?

Villas of The Mind

They live upon capital in the hope that the sum of things will hold together for their lives, and beyond that they do not care what happens. They may regret the decline of their country, but the pain is short-lived. They take refuge in Roman villas of the mind. "Oh yes, things do seem pretty bad," they say. "But trust old Winston —he'll see us through." The aura around "old Winston" is so dazzling that it quite blinds them to the fact that he now does what he declared he would not do—presides over the liquidation of the British Empire. They are grateful for that dazzle. They are grateful for anything that shelters them from the perception of reality. They do not wish to exert themselves, to make the slightest call upon their moral courage. They are decadent.

Others, while certainly not personally decadent, nevertheless accept decadent values. They ask with a gesture of despair: "What can I do about it?" Tell them they can at least master and make known the facts, and they look at you with sad eyes, as though you were putting forward impossible demands, and seize the first opportunity to tell you about some good batting at Lord's or a fine pass at Twickenham. They are quite sincere in their belief that they are powerless to affect the issue. Others again feel that they do all that can be expected of them by fighting popular causes. Fighting Soviet Communism, for instance. There are plenty of cheers nowadays for doing that. But suggest that they should also fight the subversion inspired by New York and their response will be very different.

Though you prove your case to the hilt, and they accept it, they will still raise horrified hands at the idea that they should fight the Money-Power which is rapidly destroying us. "My dear fellow," they exclaim, "it would not be popular." Consciousness of having fought in one or other or both of the world wars prevents them, very often, from stopping to think how cowardly an attitude that is: Have they not proved their manhood in battle? But in time of war the whole national sentiment is on the warrior's side. That is a very different thing from carrying on the kind of struggle in which *Candour* and its friends are engaged — a lonely struggle, dedicated to the facing of unpopular truths and conducted in the teeth of derision and hostility. The wind that blows from Siberia is so cold and icy that only the exceptionally brave of spirit and honest of intellect will thank one for pointing out that Wall Street offers but illusory protection from the blast and that the only hope for the British people lies in the resurgence of British power.

"Pure nineteenth century, my dear fellow," they tell you. "We have outlived the days of imperialism." In our modern world, which has witnessed the rise of the great empires of New York and Moscow, that argument is almost comic.

* * * * *

In spite of long years of ministerial misrule and policies of surrender, we still possess an Empire, and this contains almost every raw material known to mankind. Huge areas of it are neglected and depressed. Intensive cultivation would bring them prosperity and at the same time enable Britain to cut completely adrift from the international dictatorship of Gold.

The Dominions, if offered second call on the British market, could not afford to withhold their co-operation, while the Colonies would be only too thankful to be incorporated in a system which aimed at their conscientious development and fair distribution of the immense wealth contained in the Imperial heritage, and they no less than we would be overjoyed to find release from the inconceivable exploitation of the Money Power.

It can be done. It must be done. It shall be done. Because the alternative is eclipse.

BEWARE THE MONEY POWER

A Warning to the British Nations

by

A.K. Chesterton

WHY THIS BOOKLET?

This booklet is the third in a series intended to serve a dual purpose. Through these booklets readers will be introduced to the policy of *Candour*, the British Views-letter, which espouses the British Imperial cause. Indeed, the contents of this booklet are the substance of articles published in *Candour*, and of other articles written by the same author for other publications before *Candour* came into existence. This series will also make clear the reasons which have led to the formation of the League of Empire Loyalists, and the aims of this devoted band of patriots who are pledged to serve the British future by maintaining a relentless opposition to internationalists known to be intent upon enslaving the world through Communism or through debt.

The *Sound The Alarm* series is dedicated to R.K.J., the animator and inspirator of this new movement.

A K C.

THE EMPIRE OF WALL STREET

Amid the confusions of the post-war world there have emerged two immense facts which are not in the least confused the power of the United States of America and the power of the Union of Socialist Soviet Republics.

Both are concealed Imperialisms which threaten the integrity of every other nation. The stranglehold of the United States is exerted by means of the subtlest and most effective of all forms of dictatorship—usury. Russia relies, in countries beyond the range of her forces of occupation, on organised fifth columnism, which makes a bid for control through direct political action and sabotage.

It is not America as such which seeks the disintegration of the British Empire, and which exerts a blackmailing pressure to that end, but the sinister power of the international money-lending racket. America enters the picture only in so far as her Government and its affiliated organisations may be prepared to act as agent for the world's financial dictatorship established in New York.

Britain faces the future with two vast and virtually self-contained nations—each inhabiting a great area under its own political control—contending against her for world power and influence. She can meet this illimitable new challenge only as an economically integrated Empire: left to her own economic and strategic resources she would become increasingly poorer and more impotent, until finally driven out of business and made an island slum appendage to Moscow or New York.

The Bolshevization of Britain is many a day's march away, but the "Americanisation" of Britain is already knocking at the door. That ardent young Conservatives should be the first to want to shout:

"Come in" bodes ill for the future of our land. Unfortunately, political realism is not one of the gifts with which our admirable people are endowed. Those of them who sense the menace of Soviet expansion are comforted by the thought of an American Galahad available to rescue all damsels in distress, while those who suspect that the American Galahad is neither as benign nor as disinterested as he would like to appear for the most part wish to rush screaming into the arms of the Soviet Union. Others again think all will be well if only they can establish a World Government.

The innocent gentlemen of Chatham House—the home of the Royal Institute of International Affairs—and the guileless professors of the microphone, who supply in all good faith the idealistic façade for the projected international dictatorship never seem to have given thought as to who the international dictators are destined to be. The Press displays a like innocence.

Idealists Who Can Do No Wrong

When it was first proposed that we should be submerged in Federal Union, for instance, *The Times* approved and *The Observer* devoted five columns to the enthusiastic support of the proposal, which was sponsored by the late Lord Lothian, then representing at Washington the King and Country whose sovereign rights he proposed to destroy. And, of course, Lord Beveridge was the prophet, priest and architect of the New Order.

To advocate handing over our national sovereignty to Germany would rightly have merited a charge of high treason; even to be suspected of wanting to do so would have been to incur the risk of detention without trial. Yet to advocate the surrender of that sovereignty to an international junta is to find the big guns on one's side and to enter into an alliance with the B.B.C., pretty nearly the whole of the Left, and a large and most influential part of the Right. It is in fact to belong to a highly fashionable Fifth Column, and to preach a form of treason regarded as distinctly honourable by the law.

While Britons were dying in battle, a pamphlet appeared in Britain demanding the overthrow of the national sovereignty for which they were giving their lives. It was signed by a big group of Left-Wingers headed by Sir Richard Acland, whom the newspapers were delighted to publicise, and including the late C.E.M. Joad, to whom almost unique opportunities were given to make known his views. The fact that they enjoyed privileges, let alone immunity, is doubtless to be explained by their unconscious loyalty to the effective masters of the situation who work behind the scenes, and whose interest is to wipe out all traces of national consciousness from the minds of the people.

* * * * *

The truth of the matter is that the Aclands and others of that sort are sincere idealists — and dupes.

Let a more authentic voice speak:

Sir Victor Sassoon was reported in the *Glasgow Herald* of June 19th, 1941, thus:

"Sir Victor Sassoon, British merchant banker, who arrived in Los Angeles yesterday, en route to Shanghai, said there was no other way to stop Hitler but to form a world federation of democracies, with Britain, Canada and Australia becoming part of the United States. "'The United States,' he said, 'needs Britain, Australia and Canada to consume the exports of South America.' "'It is now obvious,' he added, 'to business men of the world that the federal alliance of Britain is so necessary that it hardly bears discussion. "'Britain must come into the democracy of the United States with full rights of

Statehood.' "'It is also obvious that such an arrangement would mean that Britain will relinquish her traditions and institutions of Government.'"

Such a renunciation would doubtless not mean a great deal to this "British merchant banker," whose family comes from the relatively distant English shire of Baghdad and whose interests were mainly concentrated in the still more distant English county of Shanghai, but it does mean something to the men of Ypres and Gallipoli, to the men of Alamein and Tobruk.

* * * * *

The Left Wing almost to a man are ready to abandon national sovereignty in favour of Federal Union, or any other shoddy little Utopian day-dream, not seeing that, these schemes are designed to cloak the underlying reality that international finance is anxious to create a world debt-collecting agency in the form of an international atomic army, which would make national resistance to the will of the cosmopolitan bankers an impossibility.

The failure of the British Press to give this matter adequate ventilation leads one to deduce that in many authoritative quarters fear of America takes precedence over concern for the Empire's future; and this in spite of the certainty that without Imperial economic co-operation Britain as a great power must cease to exist.

The International Minority

Strictly, however, it should be recognised that the vast majority of Americans are innocent of any desire to reduce our country to the status of a vassal state. For their own national sovereignty is as much threatened as is ours. *The people to blame are those who seek to compensate themselves for their own lack of roots by controlling in usury the entire habitable world.*

In reality Empire economic co-operation has been forbidden by the financial dictators who control the world, and who are determined upon the progressive exploitation and enslavement of mankind through usury. Unless we contract out of the international financial system we shall beyond doubt lose the Empire altogether, for left and right the assaults upon it are being pressed home under the aegis of the Money Power.

NATIONS IN REVOLT

The assault upon British sovereignty is no new thing; it began thirty-six years ago, when we emerged in triumph from the first war, to find that the centre of financial power had moved across the Atlantic, taking with it a large measure of control over our national destiny.

We had preserved our independence against the German onslaught only to hand over a large slice of it to Wall Street. Henceforward we were not to be complete masters in our own house: indeed, the extent to which we abrogated "sole sovereign sway and masterdom" is to be gauged by the dropping of our historic claim to supremacy on the seas, by the non-renewal of the Japanese Alliance, by the disastrous return to the gold standard, by the pay cuts—dictated by New York—which led to Invergordon, and by that famous loyalty to Geneva which proved that we were even more enslaved by the Money-Power than were the citizens amongst whom it had set up its headquarters.

There seemed for one wild and splendid instant in the 'thirties the possibility that industrial capitalism, represented by the Federation of

British Industries, might rebel against the dictatorship of finance capitalism and so set itself and the nation free.

The creators of wealth, even in their highest councils, began to question the rule of their masters —those useless parasites who create nothing but debts. They dared the uttermost pinnacle of heresy by restating—although not in public —the truth that the essence of trade is barter, not the movement of goods about the world to pay interest to the international financial houses. But the moment passed, the vision faded. Whips cracked and the industrialists, following the new tradition of British leadership in every walk of life, cringed and came to heel.

Now they are more deeply sunk in their servitude than ever before, as their recent document, *The World Bank*, all too miserably attests.

* * * * *

In 1944, when the hearts and minds of all decent people were directed upon the world's agony, the word went forth that now was the time to take advantage of the general preoccupation by laying the foundation stone of the post-war financial structure, to ensure that although the whole of the rest of mankind be defeated, the master-usurers would be guaranteed the fruits of victory.

The Allied Governments, made craven by their dependence upon the powers behind Morgenthau, Secretary of the U.S. Treasury, obediently sent their experts to Bretton Woods, where they acted as midwives at the birth of the International Bank for Reconstruction and Development. Few of the experts, least of all Bloomsbury's White Hope, the late Maynard Keynes, are likely to have had the faintest suspicion of the true implications of that Final Act—grim title— which was to give international finance an open and official status in the new international order.

Pay Tax to Borrow Back at Interest

There was this much to be said for the old mediaeval usurer. By whatever means he extorted it, the money which he lent came out of his own purse. There was this much to be said for his successors, the "Dutch" financiers who were behind the creation of the Bank of England. The money which they lent, or on which they based their swollen credit system, was normally money voluntarily entrusted to them. But the "American" financiers, shaken by events in the 'thirties and determined that they should not recur, thought of something better—to have their security deposited in advance in the shape of gold and national currencies subscribed by governments from national exchequers. Nations, in other words, were to be taxed for the funds which the International Bank would advance. International money-lending *de luxe*!

This, I admit, is putting the position roughly and even brutally. Apologists for the Final Act of Bretton Woods will raise supercilious eyebrows and enquire whether I am unaware that there are fifty-four member-countries who run the show. That may sound impressive enough, but how many of those countries are in debt to America, and how many of those governments are in the queue for more American loans or grants-in-aid?

Over nine-tenths of the loans made by the Bank have been made in dollars. Is it really supposed that the slick bankers of New York, backed by this overwhelming preponderance of the dollar subscription, do not call the tune? Or are they good little democrats anxious only to serve the will of the majority?

Universal Cartel

The International Bank has not yet got into its stride. Its advances to date amount to little more than $1,800 million. But it is already the nucleus of a potential world money trust and nothing is more probable—unless the world revolts —than that at the next step it will disclose as its objective the attainment of a position which would make it not only the sole dispenser of international financial patronage but the only permitted source of the world's economic power in every other sense, including the effective ownership, through international consortiums, of world supplies of uranium, oil, chemicals and other basic raw materials.

Its attempt to insinuate itself into the control of the Persian oil industry was one pointer to its ultimate aim of securing for organised finance capitalism—in other words, the Jewish, Money Power—the economic sovereignty over mankind which it so manifestly desires as the pre-requisite of full political domination.

Remember who it was who financed the Russian Revolution of 1917. It was a collection of "American" financiers with their hangers-on. Among their objects in pursuing that policy was the ruination of the British Empire. Remember, too, that Roosevelt was as thick as thieves with Stalin, while treating Churchill as a lackey. Eisenhower smarmed over the Russians by telling them that they, in common with the Americans, were free from the taint of that Imperialism which disfigured the name of Great Britain.

As New York Jews during the first world war financed Trotsky, so in the second world war did New York Jews direct UNRRA supplies in vast quantities into the areas over which Communism had been extended. These supplies served two purposes: they helped to buttress the economies of the two countries behind the Iron Curtain and so enable the new regimes to weather the difficult period of transition, and they fed the vast migration of Jews from Eastern Europe to Palestine. The meticulous organisation of this trek, involving the complicity of almost every European government, as well as the United States administration and army, was so secret that the British public knew nothing about it until one day long after it had begun General Sir Frederick Morgan blurted out the truth.

Here, as every disinterested student of affairs must agree, is proof positive of the existence of a supra-national body exercising hidden power on a world scale. Hence the attack on national sovereignty in general and the assault on the British Empire in particular.

The quandary in which Britain finds herself is one of the utmost difficulty and menace. Any attempt to steer her own course by building up an Empire economy on a sane monetary basis would meet with immense opposition abroad, and be freely sabotaged at home by Fifth Columnists—both those serving Moscow and others on the right who seek to shelter behind the illusory aegis of America.

Before the last war, in January, 1939, writing in the *New Pioneer*, I made the following plea for last moment sanity:

"The authoritarian States, by fighting the money-juggling racket on all its innumerable fronts, have been able to achieve prodigious feats in reconstruction, while the infinitely richer lands of Britain at home and beyond the seas have become in large part so much urban and rural slum property.

There should be no need to stress the moral—the organisation of British self-sufficiency within an Empire economic system.

But not only are vast sums of money spent on propaganda to keep the British people in slavery to the Money Power; the most active measures are now being taken to condition these loyal slaves to act as policemen against the rebel nations, the crushing of whom would be a victory only for the Lords of Gold.

It has been observed that these new Imperialists of Wall Street and the City of London are mostly of the Jewish race. That is a misfortune, because it confuses the issue in the muddled minds and tender hearts of our people. It does not matter to what race the conspirators belong. Be they Jew or Gentile it is an abominable wickedness that a war should be so much as contemplated on behalf of the most shameful nest of parasites ever to spread desolation and misery over the face of the kindly, bountiful earth.

Let us have done with this evil thing and acknowledge no longer the sovereign power of finance to rule our lands. Instead, let us return to the Empire won for us by the intrepidity of our ancestors, and which a million brave men only twenty years ago died to defend."

Hitler's revolt was not mild. It challenged the entire concept of international lending and established as a basis of trade the mutual exchange of goods, without recourse to the usurers. There had been pioneers before Hitler. Kemal Ataturk had carried through the reconstruction of Turkey without borrowing a penny from abroad. Mussolini had safeguarded Italian currency against foreign speculators and striven as far as possible to build up for his own people a self-contained economy. He was to have successors in Spain and Portugal.

After the emergence of Hitler, however, it became clear that the international financial system was in mortal danger and that only by another war could it ever regain control over its vast empire—the empire built and maintained by debt. As it happened, Hitler was only too ready to oblige, and war came.

The master-financiers of America, and their associates elsewhere, breathed again: now they would be able not only to retrieve all the ground they had lost, but, by careful planning, to ensure that such rebellions never again occurred, or —if they did occur—that they should be put down by inter-national armed force.

Taking No More Chances

As in 1913 they had grafted their wicked designs upon President Wilson's idealism to secure their precious central banking system, so in 1919 they had done precisely the same thing to secure that "hope of all ages," the League of Nations. One of the first actions of the League was to recommend all member states to return to the gold-standard, which leaves little room for doubt, even if no other evidence were available, that it was from the beginning the kept creature of the Money-Power.

Geneva, however, was a sad disappointment to its promoters. When the opportunity came to coerce the rebel nations, "not a ship, not a gun," was available for the job. Next time the chosen instrument should have "teeth" to enforce the Wall Street writ. This was decided long before the war came to an end—at Dumbarton Oaks.

The war was to fulfil everything else that had been expected of it. The first rebel to be brought to heel was Great Britain, whose foreign assets were taken over by New York almost *en bloc*. Thereafter, as we shall see presently, much more ambitious plans were prepared to ensure her complete subjection to Wall Street.

THE CONQUEST OF RUSSIA

After the appearance in the *"Weekly Review"* of my articles entitled "Britain's Alternative," in which I drew attention to the line-up between international capitalism and international socialism, a reader wrote to say that she could not on any account accept my thesis. Why should men who achieve success under capitalism, she asked, be so foolish as to subsidise revolt against capitalism and so cut their own financial throats? Clearly my

correspondent had still to discern behind capitalism and socialism the ruthless men who make use of both for their own purposes.

Perhaps the best answer to my sceptical correspondent was that given to the Compte de Saint-Aulaire, one time French Ambassador to the Court of St. James, by a New York banker who had financed the Communist revolution in Russia in 1905 until its final triumph.

Said the banker: "Marxism, you say, is the bitterest opponent of capitalism, which is sacred to us. For the simple reason that they are opposite poles, they deliver over to us the two poles of the earth and permit us to be its axis. These two opposites, Bolshevism and ourselves, find themselves identified in the International. And these two opposites, the doctrines of the two poles of society, meet in their unity of purpose, the renewal of the world from above by the control of wealth and from below by means of revolution."

Mr. A. N. Field, who has done more than any man living to expose the wickedness of the financial system, summed up in these words the situation as it existed in 1932: "The position is that international finance, by enticing the world into enormous debts and then withholding the means of payment, is goading mankind into the arms of the international revolutionaries established in Moscow."

Kings Versus Financiers

One popular fallacy should at once be exploded—the fallacy that this "imperialism of capital" has been set up in the teeth of Left-Wing opposition.

The contrary is true.

Revolution throughout has been the friend and ally of finance-capitalism. Whether or not the French Revolution increased the sum of human liberty, equality and fraternity offers a subject for debate, but there can scarcely be any debate about its one concrete fact, which was the sweeping away of the Monarchial State and the founding in place thereof of the Bankers' State.

The Revolution of 1848 brought precious little happiness to ordinary human beings, but out of it arose the central banking system of Germany, which reached its apotheosis under the Weimar Republic, when financiers achieved more absolute power than they had ever before enjoyed. The Russian Revolution, which furnishes a complete picture of the international relation between international capitalism and socialism, will be considered later. Some account must first be given of the way finance works.

The technique of money-lending on its simplest level is to make an advance against security, draw interest and at an agreed date receive back the capital sum—other things being equal, a perfectly honest transaction. If the more ambitious money-lenders kept to this even routine, however, they would be a very long time attaining power. What they desire, therefore, is that the money they lend shall either be repaid to them when its buying power has been greatly enhanced, or that it shall not be repaid at all, thus enabling them to foreclose on their mortgages and become possessed of their victim's capital assets.

These two *motifs* have long determined the course of economic history, explaining slump and boom, and enabling a small band of international lenders and manipulators to become the virtual masters of the world.

If a group of men in any country wishes to secure financial control over that country's destinies, the most obvious initial step is to gain control of the issue of currency. This involves two cardinal principles—a single, controllable currency basis, such as gold, and a monopoly of the right to circulate notes and otherwise issue credit on that foundation.

The banking history of the United States shows how the manipulators went to work to attain these objectives. Their weapon in every case was a deliberately engineered Stock Exchange panic, bringing ruin upon thousands of honest producers. In 1890 there was in America a monetary stringency, to counteract which the Government three years later introduced the Sherman Silver Purchase Act, providing the means, by Government purchases of silver, of preventing currency contraction. The financiers moved swiftly into battle. This threat to gold, their chosen medium, could not be tolerated. The American Banking Association circulated to members instructions to sabotage the Government's plan: —

"Silver, silver certificates and treasury notes must be retired," ran its fiat," and national bank notes upon a gold basis made the only money. This will require the authorisation of 500 millions to 1,000 millions of new bonds as the basis of circulation. You will at once retire one-third of your circulation and call in one half of your loans. Be careful to make a monetary stringency among your patrons, especially among influential business men. Advocate an extra session of Congress to repeal the purchasing clause of the Sherman Law."[4]

Even at that time finance enjoyed a measure of international power, for India was brought in to help the campaign, which she did by stopping the minting of silver. This, in conjunction with the panic deliberately induced by the New York bankers, caused the closing down of silver mines, the shutting of factories, the crashing of banks, widespread ruin—and, of course, the repeal of the offending Act. Gold henceforward was to be the sole basis of currency, as the bankers had planned.

---

[4] Fifty years later this circular was declared to be a forgery, but nobody challenged it when Mr. Chas. A. Lindberg brought it to the notice of the House of Representatives in 1913. In any case, it describes precisely what did happen.

While crashes of this diabolical kind had often, as here, a political motive, it is to be noted that those at the heart of the conspiracy invariably managed to turn the chaos to their own immense financial advantage. One direct result of the 1893 panic was the transference of the Union Pacific Railroad into the hands of Jacob Schiff, head of the banking firm of Kuhn, Loeb and Company—to-day the monarchs of international finance. A few years later, moreover, Schiff managed to bring the mighty Great Northern Pacific Railway crashing to the ground, and from the ensuing panic his firm emerged as the complete masters of American railway finance: through Northern Securities Company it controlled £264,200,000 worth of stock and became an acknowledged member of the Money Trust which dominated the entire field of American Capitalism.

* * * * *

Jacob Schiff was now to be joined in Kuhn, Loeb and Company by Paul Warburg, scion of one of the great German banking families, and together they moved forward to the attainment of the second objective—control of all currency through a central banking system. In 1907 there was another great crisis when the Knickerbocker Trust failed, not because of any general panic action by the ordinary investor, but because manipulators of the millionaire class wilfully created a run on the banks. From this debacle they emerged incomparably more powerful, having bought up the stock of the ruined victims, which they held to re-sell at par. At the same time the Steel Trust was able to complete its absolute monopoly. It may or may not have been a coincidence that Solomon Loeb, of Kuhn, Loeb and Company, was a member of Knickerbocker Trust. At any rate, the attainment of a central banking system was brought very much nearer to fulfilment—that consummation so devoutly wished by Kuhn, Loeb and Company.

Suspiciously Obliging

Appalled at the ducks and drakes which were being played with the money-system, many genuine idealists in the United States—chief among them Woodrow Wilson and William Jennings Bryan, that doughty foe of the Money-Power—determined upon large-scale reforms to create order in place of the prevailing brigandage. And it so happened that there was a gentleman at hand only too happy to help them. His name was Mr. Paul Warburg!

What did they want? To secure stability in the price level? Why, Mr. Warburg had the precise specific up his sleeve—a Federal Reserve System which would hold reserves centrally and dispatch supplies of credit at once to any necessitous bank in the system that might call for them.

His plan, in most essentials, was the one adopted, and on December 20th, 1913, Mr. Carter Glass, sincerely denouncing the old laissez-faire order, secured the passage through the House of Representatives of the Federal Reserve Act, the vital clause of which when the Bill was introduced was a provision for the fixing of the discount rate to promote stability in the price level. How ironical it was, therefore, that when the Bill emerged these words: "To promote stability in the price level" were surreptitiously dropped!

At subsequent investigations officials of the Federal Reserve Board even denied that such had ever been its function.

Two years later, Sir Cecil Spring-Rice, our Ambassador to the United States, placed on record the fact that the group of financiers associated with Kuhn, Loeb and Company had become supreme in America, and that Paul Warburg was the Federal Reserve Board! William Jennings Bryan lived long enough to stand aghast at the horrified thought of what his name, in all innocence, had helped to bring into being, but no such shame cast a shadow on the happiness of

Warburg and his friends, who now had exclusive power of note issue to the reserve banks, as well as power to fix the discount rate, which meant, of course, power to determine the amount of money in existence. They had conquered America: they were now ready to conquer the world.

It has been suggested that revolution is a good friend of finance-capitalists, but they have an even better friend—war. War makes them the dictators of mankind. How lucky for them that, the year following the setting-up of the Federal Reserve Board, a war should duly arrive to complete their happiness! War has several advantages. It places the nations engaged therein in urgent need of credits, which the financiers can be-stow on their own terms.

It unsettles things, making it easier to change the masters of a people. And in this particular war it seemed likely that many kings would lose their thrones—a pleasurable thought for those who opposed to the Monarchial State the larger beatitude of the Bankers' State.

In particular, the Kuhn, Loeb bankers had their eye on one monarch whose head above all others they wished to see rolled in the sand—the head of the Czar of all the Russias.

Why It Was Safe To Let Britain "Win"

That is one reason why, in 1914, they were so ardently pro-German and so hostile to Britain. The Bolshevik Revolution of 1917 changed all that. Simple people imagine that the Russian Revolution was a protest against just such a system of wicked financial manipulation as I have described. What would be their surprise if they knew that the Bolsheviks were directly subsidized by—can you guess?—Schiff, Paul Warburg, Max Warburg and the entire Kuhn, Loeb and Company outfit! The first war objective, therefore, was gained when Imperial Russia fell.

There was no longer the same reason for hating Britain, especially as Britain had done that which arouses love in the hearts of all true money-lenders—got hopelessly and inextricably into their debt. The late Lord Reading negotiated with the United States a loan of £1,000,000,000 which that optimistic gentleman promised that we should repay on demand—and in gold! Thereafter there was no need for the Schiffs and the Warburgs to worry about Britain: we were safely in the bag. And if the war ended with the defeat of Germany and Austria—well, that would be at least two more crowned heads out of the way of a bankers' world state. America duly entered the war on our side!

* * * * *

First fruits of the great victory, for the Wall Street financiers, was the extension of their power to Britain and the Dominions, forcing us to surrender our command of the seas, to break our alliance with Japan, and, in a very short time, to return to the gold-standard, after which their associated concerns, such as General Electric, began to acquire our capital assets.

They penetrated into every part of Europe and Africa. In China they became supreme in the international financial consortium which was formed to exploit that country. They were active in India. They conquered all South America except the Argentine. And in the United States itself they went from strength to strength by using the mechanism of the Federal Reserve Board for purposes diametrically the opposite from that for which it had supposedly been formed: that is, instead of forwarding supplies of credit when necessary to avoid a panic, they used the opportunity again and again to cut off credit supplies altogether.

By such means, in the early twenties, they encouraged the farmers under boom conditions to borrow and expand their enterprises, and then promptly called in the loans, delivering thousands into bankruptcy. Precisely the same technique caused the panic of 1929 which led to the great crash of 1931.

Orthodox economists attribute this later disaster to the failure of the Creditanstalt in Vienna, arguing that it set in motion the whole succession of breakdowns which followed throughout the world. That, however, is a very incomplete picture of the actual situation. Mr. Louis T. McFadden, Chairman of the U.S. House of Representatives Banking and Currency Committee, referring to the New York Stock Exchange collapse which began the American end of the slump, declared: "It was not accidental. It was a carefully contrived occurrence... the international bankers sought to bring about a condition of despair here so that they might emerge as the rulers of us all." Nothing could be less equivocal than that. What cannot be denied is that in 1928 the Federal Reserve Board was feverishly expanding credit to create a boom, and next year as feverishly restricting credit to create a slump.

An Easy Game For The U.S.A.

American politicians are almost without exception the agents of mighty interests which move towards defined objectives. Great Britain, no longer mistress of events, has become their plaything. Her politicians, outwitted and outmanoeuvred at every turn, have created for themselves problems of such immensity that their minds become paralysed before they even begin to search for a solution.

It is only too abundantly clear that no British politician understands the supreme fact of the contemporary world—the scientific use of power in the service of long-term national policies. The aim should be to teach our governors to find a British counter to the American system. Unless the counter be found, our leaders will continue to be mere pawns in a game which they do not comprehend, and there will be no future for Britain. Our sun will have set.

MOSCOW: WALL STREET MUTUAL AID

If the row which occurred in the United States over the appointment by ex-President Truman of the late Harry Dexter White as United States executive director of the International Monetary Fund were a purely American affair, there would be no occasion to offer any comment on a very queer business. But the facts which have come to light fit so neatly into the pattern of the world's most gigantic conspiracy that they cannot be ignored.

The facts, briefly, are these: White—the family name at one remove is said to have been Weiss —while serving as Mr. Morgenthau's Assistant Secretary to the Treasury, produced under orders a blueprint for the financial domination of the post-war world. The blueprint become known as the White Plan. It gave such power to the Money-Barons, and made such deep inroads upon national sovereignty, that even the compliant British Government took fright. The result was the wedding of the White Plan to the Keynes Plan to produce the only slightly less tyrannical Final Act of Bretton Woods.

White was thus both the adroit brain behind the not very gifted Mr. Morgenthau and the nominee of the New York Money-Trust. According to Whittaker Chambers and Elizabeth Bentley, both of whom in other contexts were believed by American juries, White was also a Soviet spy. Only those whose minds are altogether innocent of the power behind governments will consider these to be incompatible functions. One of the largest Wall Street houses financed the Russian Revolution and maintained close contact with the Soviet Union throughout the inter-war period. During the war, when the ranging of Russia on the Western side made the step respectable, there was scarcely an official institution in the United States which escaped becoming an unofficial part of the Communist conspiracy.

Fifth Column In Action

Two examples will indicate the general trend. As the Anglo-American armies fought their way up the length of Italy, M. Vishinsky was permitted to follow in their wake organising the country to form part of the post-war Communist empire. General Mark Clark has placed on record that Vishinsky's activities were well known to Washington. The second example is furnished by the protest to President Roosevelt of the Polish Prime Minister that every word broadcast to Eastern Europe from America was undiluted Communist propaganda. Roosevelt promised M. Mikolayczyk he would see that it was stopped. The propaganda continued until after the war. Those who rule behind the scenes, making use of Presidents and Prime Ministers as mere puppets, willed the Bolshevization of the world. That is certain.

Communism Merely An Instrument

It is no wonder, therefore, that people like Harry Dexter White and Alger Hiss had no difficulty in serving both New York and Moscow: they served one and the same masterdom. A naïve British commentator once expressed his astonishment that Hiss should have followed a course inimical to his own career. The truth, of course, is that both White and Hiss had rapid promotion and achieved positions of great influence precisely because they took that particular course. The apparent contradiction is impossible to understand unless it be realised that the secret masters of America were—and in all likelihood remain — Communists, or at any rate, men anxious to use Communism, and whatever else may offer, to smash Christian civilisation.

The accusation has been levied against ex-President Truman that he appointed White to be American executive director of the International Monetary Fund after in-formation had reached him from the Federal Board of Investigation that the man was a Soviet spy.

When the Attorney-General, Mr. Brownell, first brought the charge, Mr. Truman was reported to have denied having read any F.B.I. report on White. Former Secretary of State Byrnes then let it be known that he had himself discussed White with the President, only to be told by him that he (Mr. Truman) considered White's Communism to be a thing of the past.

Nine long, dangerous years after Chambers had warned the United States Department, the whole poisonous conspiracy was forced into the light of day by the Committee on un-American Activities—that grossly maligned body—and above all by the pertinacity of one of its members, now Vice-President of the United States. Senator Nixon, by sheer dint of manhood, refused to allow the most powerful influences in the land to continue to shield Hiss. This clever, elegant scoundrel, after long side-stepping the probes of the Committee, landed himself in such a morass of lies that the Grand Jury could scarcely do less than indict him on a charge of perjury.

Unwelcome Evidence

Then came the real evidence, which Chambers hitherto had been unwilling, out of a mistaken sense of mercy, to produce. Scores upon scores of copies of top-secret State documents, typed on Hiss's own machine, which he had fed into the Soviet espionage-system from his office in the State Department, were brought out of hiding and made available to the authorities. Instead of leading to a mighty surge of feeling against the exposed Hiss, it led to an unprecedented propaganda campaign against the exposer, Chambers. History has never known anything like it. President Truman entered the lists against Chambers. Two High Court judges—one of them Felix Frankfurter — went into the witness-box to give Hiss a first-class character. Even after the man stood condemned, Secretary of State Acheson, as though treason against the United States were a small matter, reaffirmed his friendship for him. The two-headed Money-

Power, in both its international financial and its Communist manifestations, had mobilised its immense propaganda resources to uphold Hiss and defame in the foulest terms the heroic Chambers. It could not prevent justice prevailing in the Courts, but it has prevented it prevailing in the minds of many men. This is something to remember when the name of MacCarthy is being universally maligned. For years Chambers felt an intolerable sense of isolation. He was Athanasius against the world.

* * * * *

What is my purpose in restating here the outlines of the Hiss-Chambers battle for truth, honour and the safety of nations? It is to suggest that in the Western world there is only one fully organised and effective international propaganda—that of the New York Money Power.

If I am right, and I am certain I am right, the implications are tremendous. It means that the mighty forces which sought to save Hiss and destroy Chambers also wanted Hiss at Yalta—in other words, they wanted the Russians brought into the heart of Europe. It means that through Hiss and Harry White they wanted to set up the United Nations and the World Bank to strengthen their stranglehold over mankind. It means that, through the Atomic Development Authority, they wanted the monopoly of power in the atomic age as they had enjoyed it in the age of gold. It means that they formed U.N.R.R.A. for the express purposes of bolstering the Soviet conquests in Eastern Europe and—at that time a related project—of financing the illegal mass migration of Jews to Palestine. It means that they willed the Bolshevization of China.

America Harbours Anti-British Movement

And, most germane of all, it means that they will the destruction of the British Empire, which we now see taking place in front of our eyes, almost without protest from a single soul.

Challenged on any one of these objectives, I am prepared to produce an abundance of evidence.

Those well-meaning but superficial observers who write to me complaining of my attitude towards America should try to understand that what I am attacking—and what, with the solitary exception of Douglas Reed, I am alone among professional journalists in attacking — is this utterly monstrous power of evil which is only lodged in America, and which would pack up and move to any other part of the world that could at any time offer it a greater leverage.

WHY WE FIGHT

We conceive our function to be the study of the organisation of international power and the exposure of every attempt to use that power for the subversion and destruction of Christendom in general and of our own British nations in particular. There is, as far as we are aware, no journal in Great Britain other than our own which asserts that the United States Government is, and has been for many years, the chief instrument used by the International Money-Power for the progressive establishment of a centralized tyranny over the Western World. That is why "*Candour*" feels impelled to maintain a perpetual offensive against it, and to interpret the major events of each week in the light of what is known of the unfolding conspiracy.

Boundless as the malevolence of Soviet Russia may be, the sober facts are that our peerless fleets, divisions and air formations have not been subordinated to Russian supreme commands but to "American" overlordship, that economically crippling measures such as our adherence to the General Agreement on Tariffs and Trade have not been forced on us by Moscow but by New York, and that Washington and the many internationalist agencies brought into being to serve the Money Power have been much more successful than has the Kremlin in destroying our Empire and other spheres of influence, to give scope for the unbridled authority of the "new unhappy lords" who aspire to rule mankind.

How then is it possible to write of the rapid disappearance of our British heritage without naming the chief instrument by means of which we are being robbed of our sovereignty and reduced to permanent satellite status? As an instance, how can one in honesty write of the latest Eisenhower-Churchill manifesto without drawing attention to the first part of the third clause which so vividly demonstrates the method of our subjugation? It reads:

"We uphold the principles or self-government and will earnestly strive by every peaceful means to secure the independence of all countries whose peoples desire and are capable of sustaining an independent existence".

Even the most advanced nations to-day have still to learn how to overcome the Money Power before it strangles them, which means that they have still to regain their full sovereign independence. What interpretation, therefore, can be placed on that sentence other than that the colonies have to be made independent only of the European nations which protect them, certainly not independent of Wall Street? Not, of course, that this is Wall Street's main policy objective, which is more concerned with weakening the metropolitan countries themselves that they may soon be shepherded into the projected international tyranny known as World Government.

* * * * *

Incredible though it be, few people on either side of the Atlantic have the least notion of the dominant politico-economic fact of our times, which is that the ruling junta in the United States has used the taxpayers' money to purchase that country's "export surplus" and distribute it abroad in such a way as to buy political power over the greater part of the world. That fact, with submission, cannot honestly be denied by anybody who has knowledge of things as they are, as distinct from the way they are made to appear in conventional political patter. The belief that hypothetical "American support of Britain and France", and not the ruthless use of the bludgeon of "aid", has led to charges of "imperialism" against the United States is sheer superstition. This is to say nothing of the employment of the same "export-surplus" to bulldoze the Western nations into conceding overall military commands on land, sea and in the air to Baruchistan's hand- selected pro-consuls.

World Government To Set The Seal

It is true that such power is not yet absolute—hence the increasing clamour for World Government —but it is sufficiently formidable to endow those who wield it with the means much of the time to enforce their decisions upon most of the peoples brought within their military and economic system. Of this signal truth *The Times* allows its readers not even a fleeting glimpse, when its Washington correspondent writes: —

"There is, therefore, a feeling that the time has come when the United States must either lose influence in the world by continuing to support policies in dependent areas of which it has in the past been the strongest critic, or else regain its position of leadership by supporting the peoples who have aspirations for independence. The latter course is considered necessary to offset Communist propaganda in Asia, Africa, and the Middle East, and some people have become convinced that the United States should go even farther and accept the obligation of active tutelage of newly independent nations, to prevent them from falling a prey to Communism. This, it is felt, may be the only way to save Vietnam, where, it is assumed; free elections would mean a Communist victory".

Here is superstition further developed. The United States, having worked unceasingly to undermine and destroy the overseas power of nations such as Britain, France and Holland and to take over the usufruct earned by those nations through the centuries, is now represented as incurring hostility in "dependent areas" by not supporting "the peoples who have aspirations for independence". If this is really what most Americans believe, and there is no reason to suppose otherwise, they must be living in a world so remote from reality that no madness which they incubate should take us by surprise.

Such suppositions nowhere impinge upon the world of fact. Yet there is method in the madness: behind the befuddled thinking of the ordinary people of America lies the clear thinking of those who contrive the befuddlement. What *The Times* correspondent really announces, although doubtless he has no suspicion of it, is a declared policy of American annexation barely concealed under the name of "tutelage".

America Backs Only Wall Street

This has already happened in many parts of the world—as, for instance, in Pakistan—and not only in so-called "dependent areas". We are all "dependants" now. But hitherto the policy has not been acknowledged. The French, having fought for eight years to save Indo-China from Communism, and having for the whole of that period been subjected to American pressure at the same time to save Indo-China from themselves, may be forgiven some grim thoughts when they learn that all this was no more than a preparation for the glorious day when the dual task would be taken over by American "tutelage".

In other words, the citizens of the United States are asked to believe, and readily do believe, that they will "support the peoples who have aspirations for independence" by making those people dependent upon themselves. At the same time they hold the no less quaint belief that they incur the suspicion of becoming "the symbol of imperialism" because of a legend that their Government backs Britain and France! Cant and falsehood thus join together to hold their revels on a truly sumptuous scale.

Meanwhile the heritage bequeathed to us, and for which we understood we fought two great wars, is vanishing. It is vanishing under the auspices of a man who declared that he had no intention of presiding over the process. Faced with the Eisenhower-Churchill manifesto, Sir Winston might say that in the sentence quoted self-government is pledged only to those "capable of sustaining an independent existence", but as he has shown by his actions that fuzzy-wuzzy tribesmen and bewildered West African negroes voting at elections for a spear or an elephant or a tree, are considered to be thus capable, he should explain which peoples in the world he believes to be unfitted for "independence".

If the sham is not apparent to the critics who complain of our insistence upon examining the policies of the Money Power and exposing the fawning subordination to those policies of our own leaders, the reason can only be that they do not want to face the blistering truth about our national and imperial betrayal.

* * * * *

The truth they dare not face is that British sovereignty, after the defeat of Imperial Germany and of Tsarist Russia, was given first priority for liquidation.

When Paul Warburg announced after the first World War that other debtor countries might hope for leniency, he made the categorical assertion that Britain would be treated as a "case apart", and so, indeed, she was treated.

During the inter-war period the New York financial bosses waged incessant economic warfare against us. Its course during the first decade can be traced in a grimly interesting book called *America Conquers Britain*, by Ludwell Denny.

Our surrender of the command of the seas and our non-renewal of the Japanese Alliance have been noted. When we called upon America for a loan to fight the ravages of the depression the terms dictated were deliberately framed to create proletarian discontent and did in fact lead to the mutiny at Invergordon. After we had found a way out of the Wall Street orbit the attacks on us were redoubled and kept up until the outbreak of war, when the assault on our sovereign independence as a Great Power had to take second place to the more urgent assault on Hitler's Reich. But it was never abandoned.

Reporting to the Legislative Assembly of the Province of Alberta in 1939, the Alberta Social Credit Board stated:

"The evidence is overwhelming that the objective of International Finance in the present struggle centred in the war is the destruction, for all practical purposes, of the British Commonwealth of Nations as the bulwark of democracy. There can be little doubt that the forces controlled by International Finance will be invoked to concentrate on the weakening of the sovereign power of the people, by means of a progressive centralisation of power. The rapid increase of the debt structure as a result of the war, the introduction of large-scale planning under bureaucratic central control, the impositions of harsh regulations and the rapid increase of taxation are methods which have already proved successful in consolidating financial control in the past under the pretext of war conditions. Therefore they are likely to be the methods used by International Finance at the present time in the pursuit of its objective of world domination..."

How lamentably true this prediction has been proved!

Get Out Of GATT

Apart from its fulfilment inside Britain, the proofs of the prophesy lie in U.N.O., in Bretton Woods, and in the special measures drawn up to give Britain the coup de grace—the American Loan Agreement, and finally, of course, G.A.T.T. Bretton Woods would have made any economic insulation of the British Empire a difficult and precarious undertaking: the Loan Agreement made it an impossible one.

Henceforward American goods and capital were to sweep us from our Empire markets. The Federal Reserve Board would dictate our financial policy during the period of the loan-repayment, meaning that it would enjoy a fifty years' usufruct of the Empire—or of what is now about to cease being the Empire—Great Britain herself being forced in repayment to sell more and more of her capital assets at home, as she has already sold them abroad.

* * * * *

If he did not become the First Minister of the Crown in order to preside over the liquidation of the British Empire, why does Sir Winston permit West Indian Ministers to be fobbed off with economic theories instead of giving the West Indies support in their struggle for existence? Why does he spurn Australia's just claim to her share of the British market? Why from the time of the Atlantic Charter meeting down to the present day does he allow his Party caucus to proclaim its adherence to Imperial Preference only as a second choice, its eyes being glutinously fixed upon the American market?

Why does he not fulfil his boast that "the trade that made Britain great shall continue and under conditions prescribed by Britain's Ministers"?

The Surrender De Facto

The chief clue to the answer, common to all these questions, was furnished by Mr. R.A. Butler when, on returning from the Commonwealth Conference in Australia, he declared his intention to work for a financial and economic equivalent to Nato — that is, for the control by international forces of Britain's very means of life. We may be sure that the sycophants and time-servers lately crowding the platform and the auditorium at the Blackpool Conference will not cheer his name any the less loudly because of that horrifying revelation of what he is really trying to do, or abate one jot of their delirious acclamation of his leader, whose approval of the Butlerian thesis must obviously be taken for granted.

What, then, is the answer itself? It is that, despite his boast, when Churchill conferred with Roosevelt at the Atlantic Charter meeting he renounced on behalf of his country all claims to sovereign independence of action. Whether or not his eyes were open I do not know; whether or not he was to become a willing or a reluctant agent of his conquerors I would not like to guess. What I do know is that throughout his political career he has taken some strange turnings and looked for advice to some exceedingly dubious quarters.

The central fact today is all too clear. There is no British sovereignty in any but the most nominal sense. There is no French sovereignty, or Dutch sovereignty, or Belgian sovereignty, or German or Italian sovereignty. Above all, there is no American sovereignty. Instead, the Jewish Money Power is sovereign. Consciously or unconsciously the

Churchills, the Edens, the Butlers, like the Spaaks, the Van Zealands, the Adenauers, are as much the creatures of the Money Power as are the Eisenhowers and the Dulleses, and as were the Wilsons, the Roosevelts, the Trumans and the Dean Achesons, the Attlees and the Morrisons.

It is the Money Power which has decreed the destruction of the British Empire, which is why the British Empire is duly being destroyed. It could not be done without the aid of the smug little gods of the Conservative Party lately acclaimed at Blackpool, instead of being hounded out of political life as fifth-columnists in the service of the most vicious and repulsive enemy which has ever clutched us by the throat.

* * * * *

Unless a great upsurge of the national spirit moves her to a speedy revolt against these iniquities, Great Britain must become a mere financial colony—slum would be a more appropriate word—of Wall Street banksterdom.

Appendix - The Life of Robert Key Jeffery

Robert Key Jeffery was born on 3rd August 1870 in Ramsbury, Wiltshire.

As far as we have been able to establish, he was one of four sons[5] born to Robert Key Jeffery and Fanny Rebecca Moon. His birth certificate reveals his father to have been a Master Mariner which explains the families' absence from British census returns, and apart from baptismal records which reveal that all of the Jeffery sons were baptised together in Liverpool in 1873, the next sighting of the Jeffery's comes in a Board of Trade Report into the loss of a ship in Chile. Robert Key Jeffery is one of the signatories. This is presumably his father, who is described as a master mariner and surveyor to Lloyds of London.

The Jeffery family settled in Pisagua, Peru[6] in 1875. This town and the region of Tarapaca became part of Chile in 1884 after the Chilean victory over Peru and Bolivia in the War of the Pacific (1879-1883). This war was fought over the rich nitrate deposits in the area.

Fanny Jeffery died in Iquique, the chief town of Tarapaca, in 1897, and Robert Key Jeffery (snr.) died in Tacna in 1904.

In 1905, Robert Key Jeffery went into business with two of his brothers in Iquique and they went on to make their fortune in the nitrate industry in the north of Chile. Sodium nitrate was used for the production of fertilisers, explosives, pottery enamels and food

---

[5] We are indebted to the Channel Islands Family History Society for much of the family history information in this appendix.

[6] Much of the information on the life of R.K. Jeffery was taken from a document written by Alfred E Jeffery. This is in the University of Bath's Chesterton collection. (File E7).

preservatives and Chile had a near world monopoly in the industry after victory in the War of the Pacific. This secured the mineral deposits and they generated a 900% increase in taxes for Chile from their newly acquired territories by 1902.

The English census of 1911 finds him in London, aged forty, and describing himself as a manager and a partner in business. It is likely that he was visiting London while managing family business affairs.

In June 1913, his brother George died, leaving R.K. as guardian of his children[7] By September of that year the children were staying with R.K. at his house in Vina del Mar. Having made his fortune, and known as "El Rico" (the rich one), R.K. decided to retire to the south of Chile, and he left for Puerto Montt in 1914.

During World War One synthetic nitrates were developed which prompted a collapse in the Chilean mineral industry, but as we know, R.K. had already made his fortune, and was astute enough to ride out the economic crisis.

In 1917, he completed a house and store in Rininahue. He returned to Vina del Mar in 1927 to sell his "beautiful house on the hill of 100 steps", and returned to Rininahue taking with him an orphan girl of eleven years of age called Maria Elba Smith.

In the early 1930's R.K. was forced to flee from his estate under pressure from the Chilean Government, and after disputes with the former Chilean president, Arturo Alessandri Palma.

He left Chile, taking with him a large fortune in bullion which he had made up into bars in Paris and settled in Jersey where he purchased four properties during the period 1933 and 1943.

---

[7] George Jeffery is recorded to have had eight children in all (Channel Islands Family History Society)

He was residing in Jersey during the German occupation, and papers in the National Archives[8] reveal that he was immensely rich. The British Treasury was compulsorily purchasing individual's gold just before the occupation and it appears that R.K. stored his gold in his house in a specially constructed strong room.

R.K. parted with his gold only after a bitter fight, and insisted on payment in Bank of England £5 banknotes. Lloyd's Bank in Jersey could not stand a draft on £80,000 and the bank notes were reluctantly dispatched from London.

He was described in the bank correspondence as "rather a peculiar person who invests all of his money in gold" and he seems to have managed to retain 700 gold Louis for travelling to and from Chile, much to the Treasury's displeasure. He may also have managed to keep possession of a matured $60,000 U.S. Government bond. The Germans arrived in June 1940.

He remained on his properties during the German occupation, although he took the precaution of sending his retinue back to Chile. He remained along with Maria Elba Smith[9] and his maid, Agustina Prieto[10] living at Uplands House, St Helier. Uplands also appears to have had a dairy farm, and R.K. describes himself as a farmer on his 1941 identification papers.

R.K. easily had £2,328 available to purchase Dielament Manor, Trinity, in January 1943, although it does seem surprising that the German authorities did not appear to question where the large sum of money came from! The Jeffery's moved to Dielament Manor during 1944.

---

[8] National Archives File T231/1304.

[9] Her identity card has her occupation as a student, and her date of birth as 27th July 1916.

[10] Alfred Jeffery refers to her as "Christina the Indian Princess" who "had guided him [R.K.] to Rininahue in 1915". She was born in Rininahue in 1905.

After the war, R.K. wished to return to Chile. His nephew Alfred offered his services as soon as normal communications were restored, and went to live with his uncle in Jersey. To smooth his return to Chile, R.K. purchased a British warship, HMS St Kilda, intending to sail it to Chile and present it as a gift to the Chilean Government which had been attempting to take over his estate claiming he was dead.

R.K. invited Arturo Alessandri and the Chilean ambassador to visit him in Jersey to arrange the legal transfer of his fortune back to Chile. The British Government cancelled the sale of HMS St Kilda just as Alfred Jeffery was about to sail it to Jersey to pick up R.K. and his companions.

The Jeffery family (made up of R.K., Maria Elba Smith[11], Agustina Prieto, Alfred Jeffery, his wife Irene and their son Peter) sailed back to South America in May 1948 on the SS Uruguay Star of the Blue Star Line. R.K. had taken the precaution of having a diplomatic passport issued to him by the ambassador. The Jeffery fortune had to be left in Jersey as the Bank of England would not allow them to take more than £5 each out of Britain.

Arriving in Buenos Aires, Argentina, the Jeffery's were met by his staff from his estate along with a jeep and money. They returned to Chile via the Bariloche Pass through the Andes. On their arrival, he sacked a Roberto Zencovitch (possibly his bastard son[12]) for financial irregularities[13]. Zencovitch went to work on the neighbouring Lacoste estate.

R.K. sold his four Jersey properties between 1948 and 1955 with healthy profits over their purchase prices. Although his 1959 will lists

---

[11] The passenger list has her occupation as a needlewoman.
[12] Information from Alfred Jeffery in the University of Bath's Chesterton collection.
[13] *Candour* 442

him as a Chilean citizen, he was a British subject until after the war. Despite his deep affection for Chile, he only became a Chilean citizen for the sake of convenience[14]. Possibly it smoothed his return to the country in 1948.

1953 saw the beginning of his involvement with A.K. Chesterton and *Candour*, and he provided tens of thousands of pounds over the next few years to fund both the journal and the League of Empire Loyalists.

In 1954, and at the age of eighty four, he sold the estate to his neighbour, Senor Lacoste, for 660,000 US Dollars. This was an enormous amount of money for the day. R.K. retained use of the estate and the premises subject to satisfactory instalments from Lacoste. He also retained some interest in the estate cattle, which were sold to Argentina.

The following year there was a volcanic eruption in the Rininahue area. R.K. was now living in Santiago, and he sent Maria Elba Smith to investigate. She made frequent visits, and in 1956/57 she returned to Santiago along with a child, and announced that she was married to Roberto Zencovitch[15].

R.K. did not approve and had a terrible row with Elba Smith (she claimed to be his illegitimate daughter, and although he never acknowledged her, it seems certain that she was) and he threw her out. Now aged eighty seven, this was a bitter blow. She had acted as his secretary and companion, and was "his Eliza". Now she had to stay hundreds of miles away.

He made a will[16] which made A.K. Chesterton his sole heir, apart from minor payments to two servants. This would have changed the

---

[14] *Candour* 442.
[15] If Roberto Zencovitch and Elba Smith were both R.K.'s children, then they were of course half brother/sister.
[16] *Candour* 408/409.

entire face of British politics by making the League of Empire Loyalists an enormously wealthy organisation, but alas, it was not to be.

On 17th April 1961, Senor Lacoste, who had the ailing R.K. staying with him in Rininahue, sent for Maria Elba Smith. She met her father, along with her daughter, for the first time since their row. Lacoste sent R.K. to hospital on 18th April.

On his deathbed on 21st April 1961, R.K. was persuaded to sign a new will, making his illegitimate daughter his sole heir. Jeffery was semi conscious at this stage and unable to sign it. His thumb print was attached instead. He died the next day.

It was not until July that A.K Chesterton discovered that his great benefactor was dead, and this only became clear after Aidan Mackey was dispatched to Chile to investigate.

A.K. instructed solicitors in Santiago to contest the new will, but before they could obtain the sealed will in A.K.'s favour that had been lodged at the Bank of Chile; it was extracted by Jeffery's lawyer on Elba Smith's instructions and handed to her. Her husband, Roberto Zencovitch, then conveniently "lost" it. As sealed wills in Chile must be opened by a court of law, A.K.'s solicitors had everybody concerned arrested on a charge of conspiracy to steal a will.

Unfortunately, the court found there was insufficient evidence of the deliberate destruction of the original will, and this decision was later upheld by an appeal court.

Although the court cases ran until 1971, the cause was ultimately lost.

R.K. Jeffery was undoubtedly an eccentric. He paid thousands of pounds to A.K. Chesterton, a man he never met. He kept his fortune in gold and he did not believe in interest because he "believed that money deposited for safe keeping should not make a profit for the owner". He is said to have kept a bath full of walnuts in case of a world walnut shortage, and he had wine substituted for water in fountains so holidays could be wetted.[17]

But above all else, he was a proud Briton who never forgot the land of his birth. He selflessly tried to ensure its survival through *Candour* and the League of Empire Loyalists.

---

[17] *Candour* no. 423

About A.K. Chesterton

Arthur Kenneth Chesterton was born at the Luipaards Vlei gold mine, Krugersdorp, South Africa where his father was an official in 1899.

In 1915 unhappy at school in England A.K. returned to South Africa. There and without the knowledge of his parents, and having exaggerated his age by four years, he enlisted in the 5th South African Infantry.

Before his 17th birthday he had been in the thick of three battles in German East Africa. Later in the war he transferred as a commissioned officer to the Royal Fusiliers and served for the rest of the war on the Western Front being awarded the Military Cross in 1918 for conspicuous gallantry.

Between the wars A.K. first prospected for diamonds before becoming a journalist first in South Africa and then England. Alarmed at the economic chaos threatening Britain, he joined Sir Oswald Mosley in the B.U.F and became prominent in the movement. In 1938, he quarrelled with Mosley's policies and left the movement.

When the Second World War started he rejoined the army, volunteered for tropical service and went through all the hardships of the great push up from Kenya across the wilds of Jubaland through the desert of the Ogaden and into the remotest parts of Somalia. He was afterwards sent down the coast to join the Somaliland Camel Corps and intervene in the inter-tribal warfare among the Somalis.

In 1943 his health broke down and he was invalided out of the army with malaria and colitis, returning to journalism. In 1944, he became deputy editor and chief leader writer of *Truth*.

In the early 1950s A.K. established *Candour* and founded the League of Empire Loyalists which for some years made many colourful headlines in the press worldwide. He later took that organisation into The National Front, and served as its Chairman for a time.

A.K. Chesterton died in 1973.

A.K. Chesterton

About The A.K. Chesterton Trust

The A.K. Chesterton Trust was formed by Colin Todd and the late Miss. Rosine de Bounevialle in January 1996 to succeed and continue the work of the now defunct Candour Publishing Co.

The objects of the Trust are stated as follows:

"To promote and expound the principles of A.K. Chesterton which are defined as being to demonstrate the power of, and to combat the power of International Finance, and to promote the National Sovereignty of the British World."

Our aims include:

- *Maintaining and expanding the range of material relevant to A.K. Chesterton and his associates throughout his life.*

- *To preserve and keep in-print important works on British Nationalism in order to educate the current generation of our people.*

- *The maintenance and recovery of the sovereign independence of the British Peoples throughout the world.*

- *The strengthening of the spiritual and material bonds between the British Peoples throughout the world.*

- *The resurgence at home and abroad of the British spirit.*

We will raise funds by way of merchandising and donations.

We ask that our friends make provision for *The A.K. Chesterton Trust* in their will.

The A.K. Chesterton Trust has a **duty** to keep *Candour* in the ring and punching.

CANDOUR: To defend national sovereignty against the menace of international finance.

CANDOUR: To serve as a link between Britons all over the world in protest against the surrender of their world heritage.

The A.K. Chesterton Trust Reprint Series

1. Creed of a Fascist Revolutionary & Why I Left Mosley - A.K. Chesterton.

2. The Menace of World Government & Britain's Graveyard - A.K. Chesterton.

3. What You Should Know About The United Nations - The League of Empire Loyalists.

4. The Menace of the Money-Power - A.K. Chesterton.

5. The Case for Economic Nationalism - John Tyndall.

6. Sound the Alarm! - A.K. Chesterton.

7. Six Principles of British Nationalism - John Tyndall.

8. B.B.C. - A National Menace - A.K. Chesterton.

9. Stand by the Empire - A.K. Chesterton.

10. Tomorrow. A Plan for the British Future - A.K. Chesterton.

11. The British Constitution and the Corruption of Parliament - Ben Greene.

12. Very High Finance & The Policy of a Patriot - Cahill & Strasser

Other Titles from _The A.K. Chesterton Trust_

Leopard Valley - A.K. Chesterton.

Juma The Great - A.K. Chesterton.

The New Unhappy Lords - A.K. Chesterton.

Facing The Abyss - A.K. Chesterton.

The History of the League of Empire Loyalists - McNeile & Black

The A.B.C. of Politics by Rosine de Bounevialle _(due December 2016)_

All the above titles are available from The A.K. Chesterton Trust, BM Candour, London, WC1N 3XX, UK. (www.candour.org.uk)